The Esso Collectibles Handbook

Memorabilia from Standard Oil of New Jersey

J. Sam McIntyre

4880 Lower Valley Rd. Atglen, PA 19310 USA

Dedication

I dedicate this book to my lovely wife, whose encourage-ment and acceptance of my hobby has allowed me to have many hours of enjoyment.

Acknowledgments

I have many people to thank for providing the material I have col-lected over the past twenty-five years. However, I particularly wish to thank those who have allowed me to photograph their collections. This material, in addition to my own, makes this book more of a complete work and consequently, more valuable to own. I would like to thank: Rich & Skeet Burris, Joe Flory, Bob Gould, Keith Knabe, W. Clark Miller, Bob Rymer, Wayne Story, Lee Terrell, Don Trammell, and Fred York.

Published by Schiffer Publishing Ltd.
4880 Lower Valley Road
Atglen, PA 19310
Phone: (610) 593-1777; Fax: (610) 593-2002
E-mail: Schifferbk@aol.com
Please write for a free catalog.
This book may be purchased from the publisher.
Please include $3.95 for shipping.

In Europe, Schiffer books are distributed by
Bushwood Books
6 Marksbury Avenue
Kew Gardens
Surrey TW9 4JF England
Phone: 44 (0)181 392-8585; Fax: 44 (0)181 392-9876
E-mail: Bushwd@aol.com

Please try your bookstore first.
We are interested in hearing from authors
with book ideas on related subjects.

Copyright © 1998 by J. Sam McIntyre
Library of Congress Catalog Card Number: 98-84275

Designed by Bonnie M. Hensley
Layout by Randy L. Hensley
Typeset in Freehand 471 BT/Humanist521 BT

ISBN: 0-7643-0518-2
Printed in China
1 2 3 4

Contents

Foreword

This Foreword has been written by noted authority Wayne Henderson. We welcome him as a contributor to this book.

Life's pursuits are many. Some pursue fame, others pursue fortune. Some pursue the exhilaration of adventure. Some of us pursue knowledge.

I've known the author of this book for most of the past twenty years. Among many friends active in the petroleum hobby, I believe he and I probably go back as far as anybody. We have always pursued knowledge. During the past years we have witnessed an entire hobby reach maturity. That maturity, the drive, the interest, has all been driven by knowledge. In the early years, there was little information. We were "junk collectors," searching old service stations for leftover "junk." With the efforts made by Sam and I, as well as select others, more and more people have chosen to join us in preserving and protecting the memorabilia of the industry that has fueled and lubricated all the progress of the twentieth century.

Some eighty-five years ago, just after the breakup of the "Standard" industrial colossus, growth in the freedom of mobility demanded the development of the gasoline filling station. Since that day, "filling stations" have taken on many images, many titles: gas station, service station, pumper, convenience store, and others. These highway icons sprang to life quickly and became the most familiar commercial sights of the era. Left in the rush of each generation's image enhancements were the artifacts of each previous era. It is these items that we pursue, that we preserve.

Standard Oil Company of New Jersey has also been known by many names. Standard, Esso, "Jersey," Exxon, and even more marketing names are known. With each "enhancement", the images common to the pre-decessor were commonly discarded...except in the memories of those of us who happened to notice. As we began to discover and collect these memories, there were always the questions...when, what, why. Our search for knowledge led us to try to answer those questions, and the book you are now holding is but one man's effort to share the knowledge he gained in pursuit of answers about his chosen company, Esso. Many others played a part...friends, co-workers past and present, collectors near and far. It could not have been done without them, and indeed that has been part of the fun—the sharing of our finds, the answers to our questions.

For those readers who are of sufficient age and who traveled anywhere in the swath from Maine to South Carolina and across Tennessee into Arkansas and Louisiana, the many Esso items shown within will seem like familiar old friends. To those from elsewhere they seem less familiar, but there are some surprises in store for you. Enco and Humble, Carter, Oklahoma, Pate, indeed Standard—with all these there is something here for you, whatever your age, wherever you are from. For our many collector friends, this work can be considered nothing less than a fantastic tribute to a popular company, the sharing of Sam's knowledge, the answers to the questions he asked. For others, employees, customers, and friends of the company, it will be a delightful look at the many items that have encouraged us over the years to enjoy "Happy Motoring" Esso style, running with the Tiger In Our Tank.

I close by repeating the "Happy Motoring" wish to all.

Wayne Henderson
Petroleum Industry Historian, Collector, Author, Publisher, and Friend!

Introduction

I have enjoyed collecting something all my life, but never anything as much as oil and gas memorabilia. I have been working for Exxon Company USA for over thirty years and have been collecting advertising items from this company and its affiliates for over twenty-five. If I have learned anything during this time it is that the company was prolific in its offerings and that it is virtually impossible to amass a collection that includes one of everything ever produced. I am continually amazed at the new things that turn up each year as I attend the various oil and gas collectible shows across the country along with other collectors. Networking with these collectors enables me to keep up with what is uncovered and then, after considerable research through my marketing library, to assign a timeline to the item. Many of the items you will find in this book have been dated in just that way. When I know the exact year I have stated as much, however most of the time I will give a more approximate date.

Each chapter begins with a brief history of the company featured in that chapter followed by photographs of the collectibles with a brief description of each. The final chapter is devoted to a grouping of several companies but follows the same guidelines as in the previous chapters. You will note that I have assigned a range of values to each item. This value represents what an item, or one identical to it, has sold for more than once over the past year.

This book is intended to provide information about collectibles from the Standard Oil Company of New Jersey and its affiliates, including items both plentiful (relatively speaking) and unique and should be enjoyed as a reference manual for both the beginner and the advanced collector. I am not attempting to establish prices for these collectibles, I'll leave that up to you to decide.

Chapter 1
Standard Oil Company of New Jersey

Standard Oil Company of New Jersey had its beginning August 2, 1882 when John D. Rockefeller and associates formed the Standard Oil Trust. During these early years it became the largest corporation of any kind in America. The official name in the beginning was Standard Oil Company (NJ), usually referred to as Jersey Standard. It was not until August 29, 1927 that the name was changed to Standard Oil Company of New Jersey (SONJ) and incorporated in the state of Delaware. Delaware was chosen because of its lenient laws regarding holding companies. The U. S. Supreme Court had dissolved the Jersey Standard Trust in 1911 and assigned specific marketing territories to each of the Standard Oils under the trust. Today the corporation is known as Exxon Company USA with affiliates around the world and is annually one of the largest corporations in the world.

Before the U. S. Supreme Court's decision in 1911, all packaged products carried the name Standard Oil Company Incorporated. If you have a can with this designation on it, you know it was produced prior to 1911. Polarine was a brand name used by all the Standard Companies before and after 1911. The dark blue color for Polarine adopted by SONJ is believed to have started in 1914.

The familiar Standard Bar and Circle trademark was established in 1924. That same year the "Standard" trademark was established. What makes this latter trademark different from that of other companies was the distinctive use of the quotation marks which was registered by SONJ. Starting in January of that year, the company began to standardize its trademarks both in letter style and color. In July they reported to all of their marketers that the Standard Bar And Circle would be used in all advertising wherever possible. The company experimented with lower case letters and different color combinations. The color combination finally decided on was a red circle and bars with the word Standard in blue capital letters. Therefore, If you find a globe lens that has a blue circle and red bars and the word Standard in red you know it was due to the 1924 brand experiment. Some product tins have Polarine inside the circle, which was also during 1924.

In the following photographs you will see some of this experimentation.

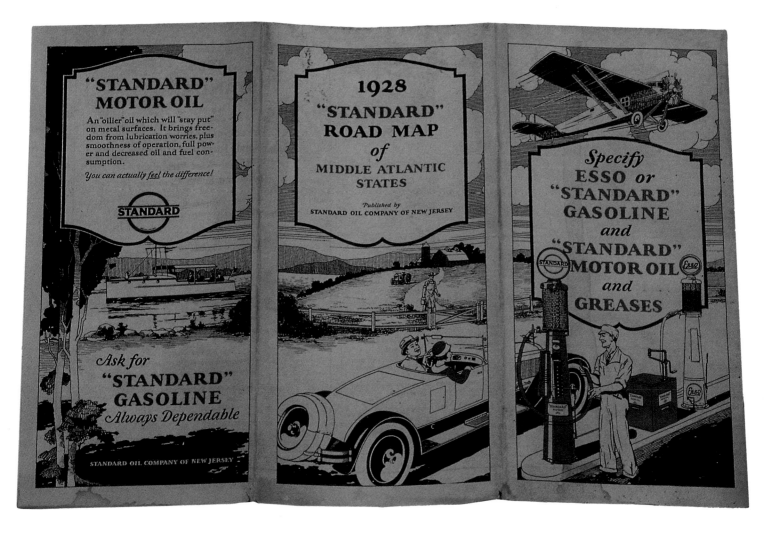

The first maps produced for Standard Oil Company of New Jersey were made in 1923. In that year only three maps were produced: the state of New Jersey, 32" x 17"; Maryland, 29" x 17"; and a small map of Virginia, West Virginia, and North and South Carolina appearing on the front and back of a format measuring 16" x 12". The Maryland map is identical to the Virginia map on the back except in a larger format.

A TYPICAL "STANDARD" SERVICE STATION

"STANDARD" DEALERS IN EVERY COMMUNITY
ALSO SELL "STANDARD" GASOLINE, ESSO,
"STANDARD" MOTOR OILS AND GREASES

"STANDARD"
PICTORIAL ROAD MAP
of
WASHINGTON, D.C.
and VICINITY

Published by
STANDARD OIL COMPANY OF NEW JERSEY

1929 "Standard" Pictorial Road Map of Washington, DC and Vicinity. This was one of the first "specialty" maps produced by SONJ.

Globes and Gasoline Pumps

Gilbert & Barker T-8 with Standard Motor Gasoline decals on the insides of the doors.
Type: 1-gallon Blind Pump
Circa: 1914
Value: $1,000-$2,000

"Standard" Motor Gasoline painted globe, 15". Metal band high profile. This globe is extremely hard to find in excellent condition. The paint was not fired on, therefore it has a tendency to pull loose and hang or fall off.
Circa: 1920
Value: $800-$1500

Standard Motor Gasoline one piece globe with chimney top, known in wide and medium width bodies. Etched lettering.
Circa: 1914
Value: $2,000-$4,000

"Standard" 15" metal band globe.
Circa: January, 1924
Value: $500-$1,000

Standard Bar and Circle lower case letters in Blue after the S. This is an example of the logo experimentation that occurred in 1924. The globe comes in 15" and 16.5". Metal band high profile.
Circa: 1924
Value: 15" $400-$600; 16.5" $500-$650

"Standard" Ethyl Gasoline 15" metal band globe. This globe is extremely hard to find. It is the only domestic globe from this company with the Ethyl logo.
Circa: 1924
Value: No Estimate

"Standard" White metal band globe available in 15" and 16.5". This was a marine gasoline.
Circa: 1920s
Value: 15" $350-$550; 16.5" $400-$625

Stanavo Aviation Gasoline metal band globe available in 15" and 16.5".
Circa: 1929
Value: No Estimate

Standard Bar and Circle with capital letters in Blue. Metal band globe. This is the letter style and color the company adopted as its logo in 1924 after much deliberation. It comes in 15" and 16.5" varieties.
Circa: 1924
Value: $350-$650

Standard Bar and Circle with capital letters in Red. Metal band globe. This was also an experimental globe even though it was registered in 1924. This is the 15" variety. I have never seen a 16.5" example but it could exist since the lower case Standard is known in both sizes.
Circa: 1924
Value: $450-$750

Cans

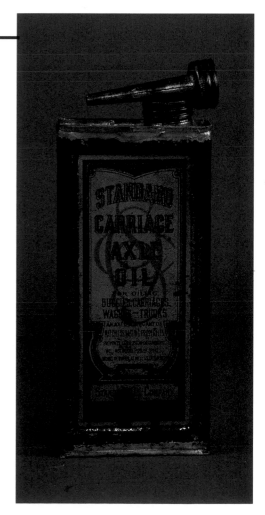

This can has the original logo SOCO superimposed on it.
Circa: 1900s
Value: $15-$30

Koto Upper Motor Lubricant.
Size: 1-quart
Circa: 1920s
Value: $10-$25

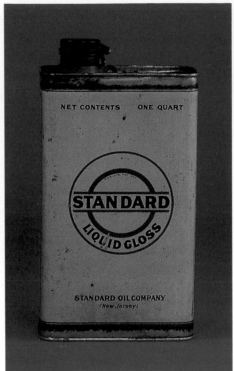

Standard Liquid Gloss. Experimental logo.
Size: 1-quart.
Circa: 1924
Value: $30-$50

Pentra Penetrating Oil. This product came in a number of different sizes. This is a very difficult can to find.
Size: 1-quart
Circa: 1910s
Value: $25-$60

Standard Penetrating Oil.
Size: 1-quart
Circa: 1924
Value: $25-$50

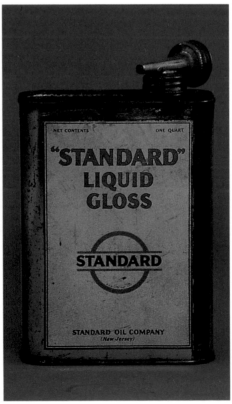

Standard Liquid Gloss. Adopted design. Product came in different sizes.
Size: 1-quart
Circa: 1924
Value: $25-$50

Matchless Liquid Gloss. This product also came in different sizes.
Size: 1-quart
Circa: 1914s
Value: $20-$50

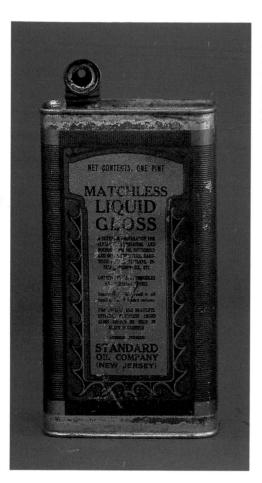

Matchless Liquid Gloss.
This can is an earlier
design than the one
described previously
and is seldom seen.
Size: 1-pint
Circa: 1912
Value: $25-$50

Standard Harness Oil.
Size: 1-pint
Circa: 1924
Value: $25-$50

Matchless Liquid Gloss with the early logo SOCO
superimposed.
Circa: 1900s
Value: $10-$30

Standard (red letters) Liquid Gloss. This was
another variety of the experimental logos of 1924.
Size: 1-pint
Circa: 1924
Value: $25-$50

Standard Separator Oil. Product came in
different sizes.
Size: 1-quart
Circa: 1920s
Value: $25-$50

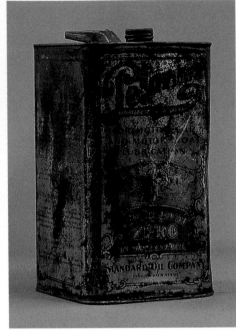

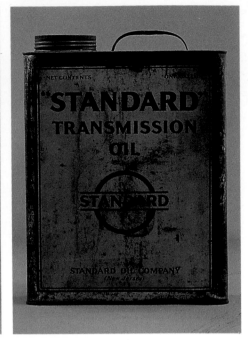

Standard Motor Oil Heavy. This product is also available in Light and Medium grades.
Size: 1-gallon
Circa: 1924-1929
Value: $25-$50

Square Polarine can. This is a tough can to find.
Size: 1-gallon
Circa: 1912-1914
Value: $40-$60

Standard Transmission Oil.
Size: 1-gallon
Circa: 1924-1929
Value: $25-$50

Nujol, a white oil laxative. Product also available in pint and quart bottles.
Sizes: 1-gallon, 3-quart
Circa: 1929
Value: $25-$35 each

Polarine can. This product was also available in half gallon cans.
Size: 1-gallon
Circa: 1914-1924
Value: $30-$65

Standard Motor Oil.
Circa: 1924
Sizes: 1-gallon, .5-gallon
Value: $25-$100, $35-$125

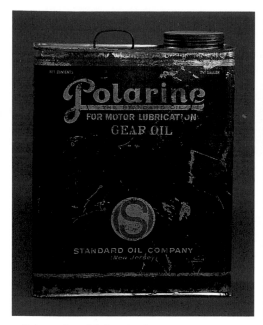

Polarine Gear Oil. Size: 1-gallon
Circa: 1914-1924
Value: $30-$65

Top center: Polarine can without Polar Bear "Will Flow At Zero Temperature".
This can has the word "Incorporated" at the bottom indicating that it came out
prior to the Supreme Court's decision to dissolve the Standard Oil Trust. In
addition, it has the old logo SOCO superimposed.
Size: 1-gallon
Circa: 1900-1911
Value: $150-$300

Top right: Reverse of the photo to its left.

Polarine can picturing car
driver and passengers.
Size: .5-gallon
Circa: 1912-1914
Value: $300-$500

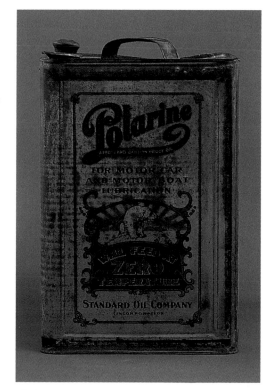

Polarine can with Polar
Bear " Will Flow At Zero
Temperature. "
Size: 1-gallon
Circa: 1912-1914
Value: $150-$300

Polarine can.
Size: 5-gallon
Circa: 1908-1911
Value: $50-$150

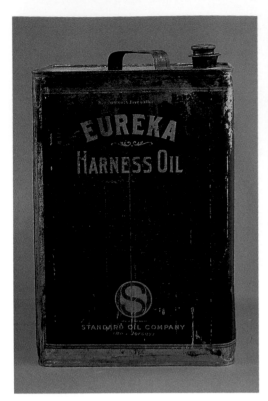

Eureka Harness Oil can.
Size: 5-gallon
Circa: 1914-1924
Value: $50-$150

Polarine can featuring car, driver and passenger.
Size: 5-gallon
Circa: 1908-1911
Value: $150-$300

Eureka Harness Oil cans.
Size: 1-gallon, 1-pint
Circa: (left) 1914-1924, (right) 1911-1914
Value: $25-$50 each

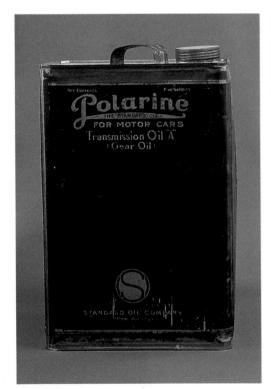

Polarine Transmission Oil can.
Size: 5-gallon
Circa: 1914-1924
Value: $50-$150

Eureka Harness Oil can.
Size: 5-gallon
Circa: 1911-1914
Value: $50-$150

Eureka Harness Oil can.
Size: 1-pint
Circa: 1911-1914
Value: $25-$50

Eureka Harness Oil can. Size: 1-gallon
Circa: 1908-1911
Value: $25-$50

Standard Motor Oil can. This is an experimental can as evidenced by the red Standard and the printing inside the circle. Note that the old Polarine logo is even used. Yes, this is an error can! The handle and the pour spout were positioned on the wrong end.
Size: 5-gallon
Circa: 1924
Value: $200-$400

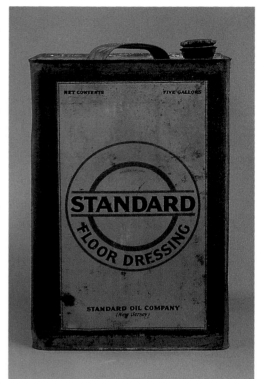

Standard Floor Dressing can.
Size: 5-gallon
Circa: 1924
Value: $75-$150

Standard Floor Dressing can featuring a man "oiling" a wooden floor. This is a tough can to find.
Size: 5-gallon
Circa: 1911-1914
Value: $75-$200

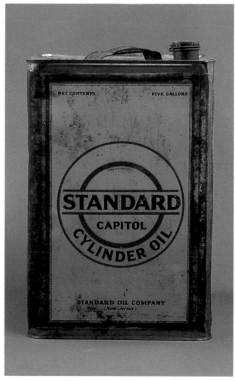

Standard Capital Cylinder Oil can.
Size: 5-gallon
Circa: 1924
Value: $75-$150

Standard Capital Cylinder Oil can.
Size: 5-gallon
Circa: 1924-1929
Value: $75-$150

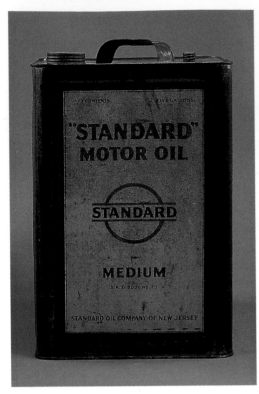

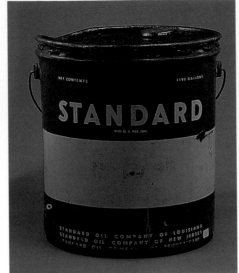

Standard Motor Oil can.
Size: 5-gallon
Circa: 1924-1929
Value: $75-$150

Standard round can used for many different products by stenciling a product name on the side. Round cans began to be used around 1930 because they were machine made and required no special handling. They were mass-produced and therefor cheaper. This is an example of an early round can because of the three Standard Oil Companies shown around the bottom edge.
Size: 5-gallon
Circa: 1930
Value: $25-$50

Aladdin Security Oil can. The lettering on this can is embossed as is the lamp. This is a very tough can to find.
Size: 3-gallon
Circa: 1885-1911
Value: $300-$500

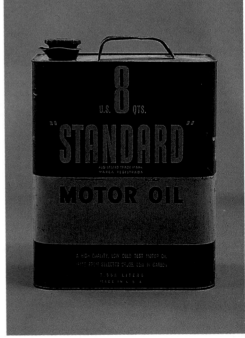

Standard Separator Oil can.
Size: 5-gallon
Circa: 1924-1929
Value: $75-$150

Stanavo Gasoline can. The Stanavo Corporation was founded in 1929 by Standard Oil of New Jersey, California and Indiana, each with one-third ownership. Standard Oil of New Jersey sold its share to the remaining partners in 1938 because they wanted to market their own brand of aviation products. Stanavo product containers and other advertising items are seldom seen.
Size: 5-gallon
Circa: 1929
Value: $150-$400

"Standard" Motor Oil can.
Size: 2-gallon
Circa: 1930-1932
Value: $25-$35

Standard Household Lubricant round can. This is a very tough can to find.
Size: 4-ounce
Circa: 1920-1924
Value: $75-$200

Polarine Cup Grease can.
Size: 1-pound
Circa: 1914-1924
Value: $25-$35

Standard Bar and Circle Household Oil round can. Tough can to find.
Size: 4-ounce
Circa: 1924
Value: $75-$200

Standard Diamond Axle Grease in a wooden box. This is a rare container.
Size: 1-pound
Circa: 1880s
Value: No Estimate

Standard Bar and Circle Household Lubricant oval can. Tough can to find.
Size: 4-ounce
Circa: 1926-1932
Value: $75-$200

Mica Axle Grease can.
Size: 3-pound
Circa: 1912-1914
Value: $25-$50

Standard Grease cans. The two on the bottom are experimental, the one at the top is the adopted design. Note the can at the bottom also has little wagon wheels inside the circle.
Size: 1-pound
Circa: 1924-1929
Value: $15-$30 each

Polarine Transmission Lubricant BB green square can.
Size: 25-pound
Circa: 1912-1914
Value: $50-$100

Polarine Cup Grease can.
Size: 1-pound
Circa: 1914-1923
Value: $25-$50

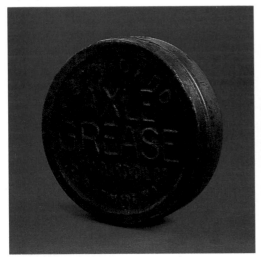

Standard Axle Grease can.
Size: 1-pound
Circa: 1900-1911
Value: $25-$50

Mica Axle Grease can.
Size: 1-pound
Circa: 1914-1923
Value: $25-$50

Standard Pressure Gun Grease can. This can came with a plug in the lid. You removed it and inserted your grease gun and sucked the grease in to fill it.
Size: 1-pound
Circa: 1924-1929
Value $25-$50

Polarine Cup Grease can.
Size: 25-pound
Circa: 1914-1924
Value: $50-$100

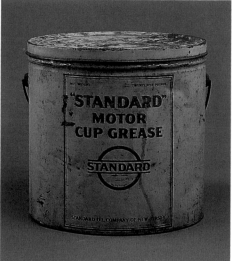

Standard Arctic Cup Grease can.
Size: 5-pound
Circa: 1924-1929
Value: $35-$60

Standard Motor Cup Grease can.
Size: 25-pound
Circa: 1924-1929
Value: $35-$65

Salesman's sample of Mica Axle Grease. The product also came in buckets similar to this one only larger.
Circa: 1906-1925
Value: $50-$75

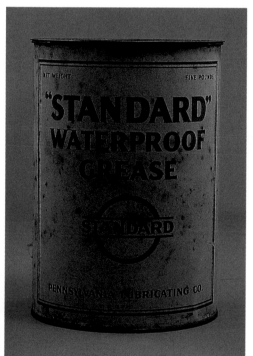

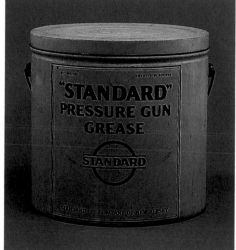

Pressure Gun Grease can.
Size: 25-pound
Circa: 1924-1929
Value: $35-$65

Standard Bar and Circle Waterproof Grease can. This product was manufactured by the Pennsylvania Lubricating Company, a subsidiary of The Standard Oil Company (NJ) located in Pittsburgh, Pennsylvania.
Size: 5-pound
Circa: 1924-1929
Value: $35-$65

General store advertising sign for Mica Axle Grease. These cardboard signs usually came in the box with the grease. You opened the box, took out your new sign, and nailed it to the wall. I suppose if you already had one nailed up, you threw the new one in the trash. Oh no!
Circa: 1900s
Value: No Estimate

Mica Axle Grease buckets with embossed lids.
Size: 25-pound
Circa: 1924-1935
Value: $100-$150

"Standard" Gear Compound
can.
Size: 25-pound
Circa: 1924-1929
Value: $35-$65

Above: Die Cut Standard Touring Service sign.
Size: 22.5" x 16.5"
Circa: 1929
Value: $200-$400

Below: "Standard" Gasoline
sign.
Size: 24" x 18"
Circa: 1924-1932
Value: No Estimate

Red Standard BB gear lube
can with Polarine in the
circle. This is another
experimental can.
Size: 5-pound
Circa: 1924
Value: $25-$50

"Standard" Gasoline driveway porcelain sign.
Size: 36" diameter
Circa: 1924-1929
Value: $200-$500

Reverse of the driveway sign.

Cast iron base of the driveway sign.

Standard Motor
Gasoline porcelain
price sign.
Size: 28" x 18.5"
Circa: 1919-1924
Value: $200-$400

Polarine For Motor Cars, Standard Motor Gasoline porcelain sign.
Size: 50" x 14"
Circa: 1920-1924
Value: No Estimate

Polarine, The Standard Oil For Motor Cars porcelain sign.
Size: 26" x 12"
Circa: 1914-1922
Value: No Estimate

"Standard" with script Esso in circle porcelain sign.
Size: 59.5" x 29.5"
Circa: 1926
Value: $150-$300

"Standard" Motor Oil tank wagon can box porcelain sign.
Size: 69" x 11"
Circa: 1929
Value: $150-$250

Standard Motor Gasoline can dispenser.
Size: 30-gallon
Circa: 1922-1924
Value: $100-$200

Standard Motor Gasoline Polarine Oil porcelain sign.
Size: 30"
Circa: 1921
Value: $200-$400

Below: Standard porcelain sign. Size: 42"
Circa: 1924-1929
Value: $150-$400

Standard Gasoline Motor Oil porcelain sign.
Size: 30"
Circa: 1924-1929
Value: $175-$375

"Standard" Gasoline porcelain sign.
Size: 36" x 18"
Circa: 1924-1929
Value: $150-$350

We Sell Standard Motor Oil porcelain sign.
Size: 36" x 18"
Circa: 1924-1926
Value: $100-$250

Aladdin Security Oil round porcelain sign.
Size: 9.25"
Circa: 1915-1920
Value: No Estimate

Polarine Oil and Grease tin sign.
Size: 28" x 12"
Circa: 1914-1922
Value: $100-$200

Authorized Standard Station porcelain sign.
Size: 18" x 18"
Circa: 1924-1929
Value: $300-$400

"Standard" Gasoline curved porcelain pump sign. This was the premium grade gasoline.
Size: 16" x 8"
Circa: 1922-1926
Value: $150-$300

Ask For "Standard" Motor Oil porcelain driveway sign.
Size: 23.75"
Circa: 1924-1929
Value: $175-$300

"Standard" Gasoline curved porcelain pump sign. This was the regular grade gasoline.
Size: 16" x 8"
Circa: 1922-1926
Value: $150-$300

"Standard" Motor Gasoline porcelain flange sign.
Size: 24" x 24"
Circa: 1920-1923
Value: $175-$300

Standard Oil Company round truck door porcelain signs, two sizes.
Size: 13.75", 10"
Circa: 1914-1922
Value: No Estimate

Standard Oil Company of New Jersey Wholesale Only porcelain truck door sign.
Size: 14" x 18"
Circa: 1924-1933
Value: $200-$400

Nuso Crank Case flushing service flange porcelain sign.
Size: 24" x 24"
Circa: 1930-1940
Value: $200-$400

Same as sign above but this one has REG. U.S. PAT. OFF.

"Standard" Motor Oil tin pump sign.
Size: 11.5" x 7.75"
Circa: 1922-1929
Value: $50-$100

Insist on "Standard" Motor Oil curved porcelain pump sign.
Size: 11.75" x 11.75"
Circa: 1921-1923
Value: $175-$300

Same as sign at bottom left but this is a flange sign.
Size: 24" x 24"
Circa: 1921-1923
Value: $200-$400

"Standard" Motor Gasoline porcelain one-sided sign.
Size: 24" x 24"
Circa: 1921-1923
Value: $100-$300

Same as sign above except this is the blue
Standard that was adopted.
Size: 4.5" x 24"
Circa: 1924-1933
Value: $200-$300

Standard No Smoking porcelain sign. This was an experimental period sign with
the red Standard.
Size: 4.5" x 24"
Circa: 1924
Value: $300-$400

Polarine For Motor Lubrication Standard Oil Co. (New Jersey) one sided porcelain sign.
Size: 18" x 24"
Circa: 1914-1922
Value: $175-$300

Polarine Sold Here porcelain flange sign.
Size: 14" x 24"
Circa: 1914-1922
Value: $200-$400

Top right: Aladdin Security Oil embossed curved corner mounted tin sign. This is a very difficult sign to find. It was used in country stores.
Size: 10" x 14"
Circa: 1890-1910
Value: $200-$300

Bottom right: Aladdin Security Oil kerosene tank. This item was found in hardware stores and shops where kerosene was sold at the turn of the century.
Size: 65-gallon
Circa: 1890-1910
Value: $250-$500

This plane is the "Flying Trade - mark"
of STANAVO, the aviation products
distributed by makers and marketers of
ESSO and "STANDARD" Gasoline.

"STANDARD"
AIRWAY MAP
NEW YORK — NEWARK
WASHINGTON
Published by
STANDARD OIL COMPANY
OF NEW JERSEY

Aviation map.
Circa: 1932
Value: $25-$50

Polarine horse chest warmer. This thick material collar hung down in front of the horse's chest in winter to keep him from catching cold and rendering him useless during the winter months. The company even got some advertising out of this item.
Circa: 1900-1920
Value: No Estimate

Standard Oil locks.
Circa: 1924-1932
Value: $50-$100
each

Dr. Seuss jigsaw puzzle. Dr. Seuss, noted children's books illustrator and storyteller, worked for Standard Oil of New Jersey from 1928-1941 and used his talents to promote the company's products. This is an example of his work.
Size: 17.5" x 11.5"
Circa: 1930
Value: $25-$100

Standard Oil locks. These locks all have special purposes. The one on the left is designed for the water drain located on the tanks. The one in the middle is to lock the gate. The one on the right is to keep non-authorized personnel from loading product. How do you tell the difference? Look at the shape of the keyhole.
Circa: 1915-1936
Value: $50-$75

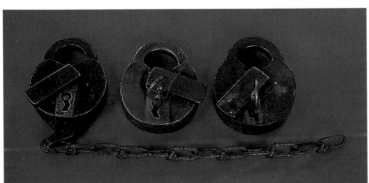

Standard Service Atlas Tire advertising poster.
Size: 30" x 52"
Circa: 1929
Value: No Estimate

Standard Parawax for home use.
Size: 1-pound
Circa: 1924-1929
Value: $10-$15

Standard barrel ashtray.
Circa: 1924-1929
Value: $25-$30

Standard pump glass add panels. The blue one is for premium fuel.
Size: 12.5" x 5"
Circa: 1923-1929
Value: $20-$30

Polarine wooden box. Most packaged products were shipped in wooden boxes during this time period.
Size: 18" x 12" x 18"
Circa: 1914-1926
Value: $25-$50

Polarine wax with applicator for the bottom of irons when ironing clothes. The tag reads " Polarine keeps your car moving," "Handy ironing wax keeps your iron moving."
Circa: 1914-1920
Value: No Estimate

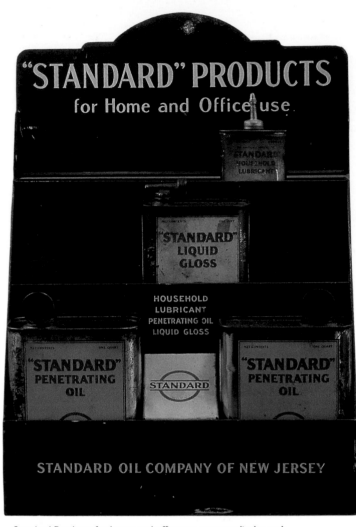

Polarine wooden box.
Size: 10" x 14" x 11.5"
Circa: 1914-1926
Value: $25-$50

Standard Products for home and office use counter display rack.
Size: 6" x 17.5"
Circa: 1928
Value: $75-$125

"Standard" Service uniform patch.
Size: 4.5" x 2"
Circa: 1923
Value: $5-$10

Standard Bar and Circle shirt and jacket patches.
Size: 6" x 5.25"; 2.75" x 2"
Value: $15-$25; $5-$10
Circa: 1924-1932

Standard uniform patches.
Size: Verified Lube 8" x 4";
Standard 4.5" x 1"
Value: $10-$15; $1-$5
Circa: 1926-1932

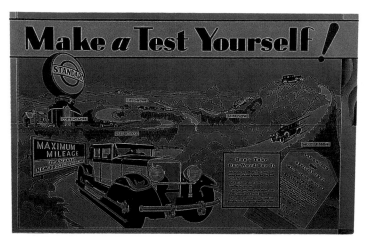

Early advertising folder.
Circa: 1924-1929
Value: $10-$20

Pratt's Deodorized Stove Gasoline tank. This product was used in stoves for cooking and was available at general stores.
Size: 65-gallon
Circa: 1890-1910
Value: $150-$300

Stanavo porcelain sign.
Size: 10"
Circa: 1929
Value: $150-$250

Above: Standard Bar and Circle First Aid kit.
Size: 9.25" x 9.25"
Circa: 1924-1932
Value: $75-$150

Below: "Standard" Gasoline pump price box.
Size: 10" x 14"
Circa: 1918-1924
Value: $150-$200

Below right: Car gas tank measuring gauges. These gauges were used to measure the amount of gasoline a driver had in his Ford T-model car. All T-models carried a maximum of ten gallons. Sometimes the car dealers would put their advertisement on the sticks.
Size: 14"-17"
Circa: 1914-1927
Value: $30-40 each.

Chapter 2
Esso

This brand had its beginning in 1926 and was originally a premium motor fuel only. It was sold in the Standard Oil Company (NJ) service stations which had begun to populate the nineteen states the company had been assigned as a result of the landmark 1911 Supreme Court decision. In 1934, all of the Standard stations were rebranded Esso due to the success of the new brand. The name Esso began to appear on motor oil and other types of lubricant containers in 1935 as a result of the first factory filled round oil cans that had been premiered a year earlier. In 1949, the company name was changed to Esso Standard Oil Company to better align itself with the brand that by now dominated all of its marketing. This name remained until 1960 when Esso Standard was merged with Humble Oil and Refining Company. However, Esso continued to be the brand name on all products in the states assigned by the Supreme Court decision and was used in Texas at the Humble stations as well.

The word Esso is the phonetic sounding of the letters S and O which of course stood for Standard Oil and have no other meaning.

Esso map.
Circa: 1934
Value: $15-$35

Esso Map of New York and New Jersey. This map is printed on silk and was a gift to employees' wives at a special business meeting held in New York in 1954. It is printed on both sides and was intended to be worn as a scarf.
Circa: 1954, Value: No Estimate

This chapter begins with the story of Esso's round factory-filled motor oil cans that began in 1934 and all the can styles that occurred from that date until January 1, 1973 when the company name was changed again to Exxon.

Esso Factory-Filled Motor Oil Cans—a Chronology

To start with, please note that I am not attempting to identify every round factory-filled quart motor oil can that Esso ever produced. As a matter of fact, except for the beginning of this history, I am not going to talk about the Essolube line of motor oils at all. This product began to occupy a lower position in the motor oil family after Uniflo was introduced and not a lot is found in company publications about the changes that were made.

Our story begins in 1926 when Standard Oil Company Of New Jersey introduced the brand name Esso to the world. The company placed this name on their premium grade gasoline and made the regular grade Standard. Eight years later, with the brand Esso gaining more and more respect and popularity, SONJ introduced its first round factory-filled motor oil can.

January 1, 1934: Essolube Motor Oil
Available in 1-quart and 5-quart cans, this motor oil sold for $.30 per quart (Fig. 1). The product had been available since August 15, 1932, but in the familiar flat, tall 1-gallon cans and bulk only (Fig. 2).

Figure 1

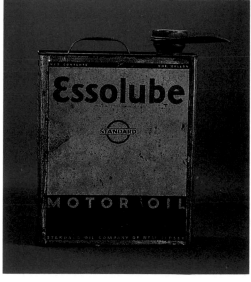

Figure 2

35

Figure 3

January 1, 1934: Essolube Break In Oil

This factory-sealed round 1-quart can was introduced at the same time as Essolube Motor Oil. It was available in SAE-20 for pleasure cars. It was also available in SAE-30 for truck engines, but not in sealed 1-quart cans. Both were available in 55-gallon light iron barrels and half barrels, and sold for $.30 per quart retail. Shortly thereafter this product was also available in SAE-10 in 1-quart cans, in a new can style. The SAE grade was omitted from the side and relocated to the tops, and " MADE IN USA " was added on the bottom edge of both sides (Fig. 3).

January 16, 1934

On this date the brand name Uniflo Winter Motor Oil was introduced by the Pennsylvania Lubricating Company, a wholly owned subsidiary of the Standard Oil Company Of New Jersey (Fig. 4). This motor oil was available in 1-quart and 5-quart cans and sold for $.35 per quart retail. This product was made available only because of the extensive work that had been done earlier by the scientists at the Standard Oil Development Company (S.O.D.), Jersey Standard's research arm, and Esso Laboratories.

Figure 4

S.O.D. developed the first motor oil additive, a pour depressant that dramatically improved low temperature starting by modifying the ever present wax crystals in the oil so it would remain fluid at lower temperatures than before. This additive was commercialized in Jersey's premium motor oil. The first additive to improve an oil's viscosity temperature properties, called "viscosity index (VI) improver," was developed by Esso Laboratories and was also incorporated in this motor oil. It was, as it says on the can, "Designed as a Winter Motor Oil," and the snow-covered tree depicted on the side of the can was emblematic of its purpose. However, the motor oil also performed well in hot climates. It replaced all SAE numbers, but made no claim to be a multi-vis product. It does say on the can that it "Combines the easy starting of an SAE-10 oil at sub-zero temperatures with the protection of an SAE-30." It had a higher VI than any oil on the market.

This product was available in two grades: Uniflo Winter Motor Oil, a 10w-20, and later Uniflo, The Low Consumption Motor Oil, which was in the range of an SAE-40 at average crank case temperatures. I might add that this identical can was also sold to the Skelly Oil Company for distribution in the west under an agreement worked out by the two companies earlier (Fig. 5).

May, 1934

Uniflo, The Low Consumption Motor Oil, summer counterpart of the highly successful premium Winter Motor Oil of the same name, was introduced. It was arrayed in the familiar red, white, and blue jacket used by Esso marketers for dressing their can family. This new oil was packaged in 1-quart and 5-quart cans and sold for

Figure 5

$.35 per quart retail. This motor oil combined the SAE grades 30, 40, 50, and 60 with one oil for both "normal" and "abnormal" driving conditions (Fig. 6). The car speeding across a picture of the sun was an attempt to demonstrate its ability to withstand the increased heat present in summer driving conditions. It was also produced by the Pennsylvania Lubricating Company, whose name had been shortened to "Penola" by this time.

Figure 6

August, 1935

Esso Motor Oil was introduced with great fanfare (Fig. 7). It succeeded Uniflo in the role of "The World's Leading Motor Oil," overshadowing its successful predecessor by the drawing power of its name and superior performance. The product was available in 1-quart and 5-quart cans in three consistencies, Numbers 1, 3, and 5 (Fig. 8). Number 1 took the place of Uniflo Winter Motor Oil. Number 3 was a new consistency for above freezing temperatures; it was equivalent to an SAE-20w in cold start-up, yet had hot cylinder wall body equivalent to the best SAE-40 oils. Number 5 corresponded to Uniflo, The Low Consumption Motor Oil.

Figure 9

The new can featured a picture on the side of an iceberg and sun, illustrating the product's flexibility in all temperature ranges. On the top of the cans, Standard Oil Company Of New Jersey, of Pennsylvania and of Louisiana were all printed in red on a white circle (Fig. 9). The word Uniflo was retained on the can but was relegated to secondary billing. Sometime between 1935 and 1939 a fourth grade was added, Number 7, which correlated to an SAE-60 or 70 (Fig. 10). During this same period, Standard Oil Company of New Jersey, Pennsylvania and Louisiana began to be embossed on the tops of the cans, instead of the early red on white circle lithograph (Fig. 11).

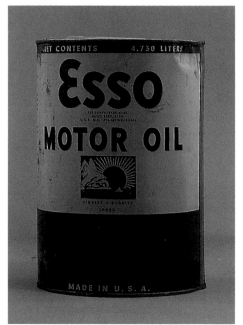

Figure 7

Figure 10

Figure 8

Figure 11

3 7

October, 1936

Essolube Motor Oil cans underwent a design change. The blue band was eliminated from the bottom band, and the can was made two colors only, a large red band at the top and a small white band at the bottom with a red dot. Standard Oil Company of New Jersey, Pennsylvania and Louisiana was embossed on the can's top (Fig. 12).

Figure 14

December, 1939: Esso Motor Oil Cans Redesigned

The word Esso was put in an oval (Fig. 13), Uniflo was moved to the side of the can (Fig. 14), the iceberg and sun were moved into the lower red band, and the word Unexcelled appeared for the first time. The oval was placed on the can to increase its resemblance to other Esso product packages and to the station identification signs.

January, 1941

Essolube HD was introduced, but was not immediately available in 1-quart cans because it was not sold through service stations. It was sold directly to the consumer wholesale. This new product was an engine oil designed for "Heavy Duty" service, particularly in diesel engines, and the HD indicates the characteristics which made it a superior Heavy Duty oil. The problem of high viscosity index and detergency existing in the same oil at the same time was overcome by the Esso Laboratories; it was a 100 VI oil, while other "Heavy Duty" oils on the market at that time were only 50 VI. The product was not available in 1-quart cans until after World War II.

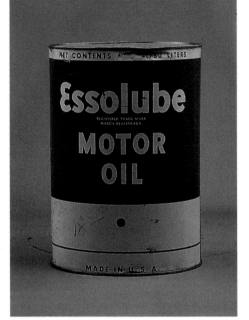

Figure 12

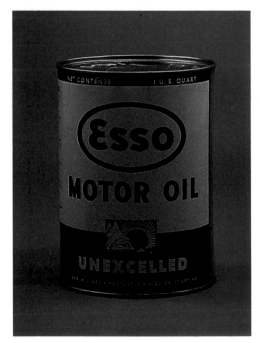

Figure 13

June, 1943

In an attempt to conserve metal for the war effort, many oil companies began to replace their metal oil cans with glass jars and bottles. Esso glass bottles were available with paper labels depicting the iceberg and sun design which had been on the cans before the war and were distributed by Standard Oil Company of Ohio in at least two grades, with Numbers 1 and 3 shown on the side of the bottles (Fig. 15). In addition, there was a different paper label bottle that carried only the name Uniflo with no reference to Esso at all. This was probably sold to the Skelly Oil Company for distribution in the west as it had been earlier. This bottle depicts the iceberg and sun design of the '30s as well (Fig. 16). Finally, there exists a regular oil bottle that was filled from a bulk oil "Lubester" with Esso in the oval and a grade designation Numbers 1 or 3 shown in the oval (Fig. 17). The bottle on the right in this figure is the one used by Esso Marketers. The one on the left also exists with the words "Standard Oil of Ohio (Distributors)" fired onto the bottle. This one was used by the SOHIO company.

January 1, 1945

Standard Oil Company of Louisiana was merged into Standard Oil Company of New Jersey. Therefore, Standard Oil Company of Louisiana was eliminated from the embossing on all can tops; only Standard Oil Company of New Jersey and Pennsylvania remained (Fig. 18).

In February of 1948, Standard Oil Company of New Jersey changed its name to Esso Standard Oil Company and all embossed can tops were redesigned to reflect this change. Standard Oil Company of Pennsylvania was absorbed into Esso Standard Oil Company on December 31, 1949. The redesigned Esso Standard Oil Company can tops eliminated Standard Oil Company of Pennsylvania embossing in 1948. Consequently, if you have a can that is only embossed with Standard Oil Company of New Jersey and Pennsylvania, you know that it was produced sometime between 1945 and 1948.

Figure 15

Figure 16

Figure 18

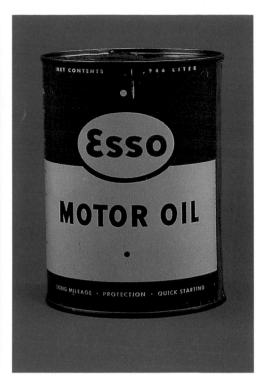

Figure 20

Figure 17

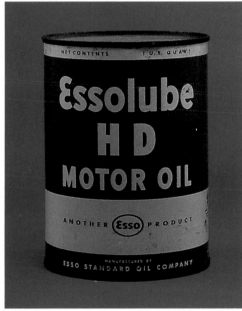

Figure 19

June 1, 1949: Esso Extra Motor Oil Introduced

This was Esso's new premium motor oil, available in five grades: numbers Zero, 1, 3, 5, and 7 (Fig. 21). As in the past, the SAE system was not used due to this oil's superior viscosity-temperature characteristics (VI) and the fact that each grade covered more than one SAE grade. The can is typically red, white, and blue with the upper wide panel being red. A new detergent inhibitor was added, which was Esso's first detergent motor oil for passenger cars.

Esso Standard Oil Company was eliminated from the tops of cans in late 1949, and was replaced with the Esso oval and appropriate motor oil grade.

June 1, 1945

Motor oil cans underwent a design change as World War II wound down. It was anticipated that product would once again be available in quart cans, instead of glass bottles.

The restrictions on can supplies were ended in September, 1945. The familiar iceberg and sun were eliminated from Esso Motor Oil cans and the color scheme was also changed. The word Uniflo was dropped, but the word "Unexcelled" was retained.

The blue color was omitted from Essolube HD Motor Oil. The new containers were red and white only with the Esso oval at the bottom (Fig. 19).

July, 1947

Esso Motor Oil eliminated the word "Unexcelled" and added a red dot on the side of the can (Fig 20).

Figure 21

Figure 22

August, 1950: Esso Extra Motor Oil Redesigned Can

The upper wide panel of the new can was changed from red to blue, and the narrow blue panel at the bottom from blue to red (Fig. 22). The color switch was based on a survey which established that blue, rather than red, is associated with premium quality. In addition, the dominating blue on the new can tied in with the blue Esso Extra gasoline pumps.

May, 1951

"A Heavy Duty Motor Oil" lithograph was added to cans of Esso Extra Motor Oil, and is found on the side of the can in white.

October, 1952

The world's first multi-viscosity motor oil was introduced. It was a new generation of motor oil, but carried the old name Uniflo. The word Uniflo had first been introduced in 1934 and was featured prominently on the first cans produced following Essolube by just a few days. Uniflo continued to be relegated to a secondary position on the cans of 1935 and 1939 but was still printed on the cans. Beginning in 1952, however, it remained the top-of-the-line automotive motor oil for Esso Standard Oil Company, Humble Oil and Refining Company, and Exxon Company USA until 1986. It was replaced at that time by Superflo Supreme Performance.

The 1952 Uniflo was an SAE 5w-20 and was actually designed for "New" or "Newer" cars that had engines with high compression ratios and close tolerances. Uniflo was recommended in particular for cars no older than 1949, although if your car was in new condition and pre 1949, it was still all right to use it.

December, 1952

The Zero and No.7 viscosity grades were eliminated from Esso Extra Motor Oil and the line was available only in Nos.1, 3, and 5.

Figure 23

February, 1954

Uniflo became available in SAE 10w-30 as well as SAE 5w-20. This new, higher viscosity motor oil was produced to meet the "Year-Round Needs of All Cars." A minor change in the can design was necessary due to the availability of two grades of Uniflo. The original red, white, blue, and gold scheme was retained but the product legend was changed and the can tops were embossed with appropriate SAE numbers of 5w-20 or 10w-30 (Fig. 23). In addition, the gold color on the new cans was more shiny, i.e., bright gold, as opposed to the matte finish gold that appeared in 1952 (Fig. 24). The 1952 can is pictured on the left, and the 1954 can on the right.

February, 1959

The Esso Oil Drop made his first appearance in the United States. This quaint figure had its beginning during World War II, when the Esso Danish company developed the character to explain the reason behind the shortages of petroleum products. The little guy soon achieved a fame all his own, and the idea was adopted in different form by the Esso Swedish company. In Switzerland, he was given the name *Quibibb Esso*. By April 1960 the Oil Drop was officially called "Happy," symbolizing the slogan "Happy Motoring" which was coined in April, 1935.

January, 1960—Beginning of the New Era

Esso Standard Oil Company merged with and officially became known as "Humble Oil and Refining Company." Beginning this year, all cans began to carry the new company name and did so until January, 1973. Naturally, they also carried the brand name Esso.

April, 1960

As mentioned earlier, the Esso Oil Drop was officially named "Happy" this month to symbolize the "Happy Motoring" slogan that had been coined in April, 1935. In 1960, motor oil cans received the slogan "A Happy Motoring Product" which appeared on all three motor oil cans, i.e. Uniflo, Esso Extra, and Esso, in the bottom color panel. Prior to this, the words "Long Mileage, Protection, Quick Starting" had appeared in the bottom panel of the Esso Extra and Esso Motor Oil cans since 1949. In addition, Humble Oil And Refining Company appeared on the opposite side of the bottom color panel. Esso

Figure 24

Extra Motor Oil received a larger word "Extra" (Fig. 25). The old word "Extra" was 5/16" high and the new "Extra" was 5/8" high. Figure 25 shows the first three cans produced that carried the new coding system, which will be discussed later.

Figure 25

May, 1961

A merger of the brand names Pate, Oklahoma, Carter, and Humble into the new brand name of Enco was completed this month. The Enco brand was used mostly in the West or everywhere that Esso could not be used. The one exception was Ohio, where only the brand name Humble was acceptable to the state. Cans were labeled with these two brand names (Humble in Ohio and Enco elsewhere) and were the same as the cans that carried the name Esso.

1962

Esso Extra changed its design to a fiber material and eliminated the red band at the bottom. The can is basically blue and white, with a red Esso in a blue oval and a 5/8" high Extra on the side (Fig. 26).

Figure 26

July, 1963

All three Esso Motor Oils were reformulated and all three—Esso Motor Oil, Esso Extra Motor Oil, and Uniflo—received new can style designs. These cans were initially issued in steel, but within thirty days were changed to fiber. Esso continued its experimentation with different can materials throughout the '60s and '70s, i.e., steel, aluminum, fiber, plastic, and combinations of these materials. Each change was characterized by a code on the side of the quart cans that that was as follows: Uniflo, S1, S1a, etc., Esso Extra, S2, S2a, etc., and Esso Motor Oil, S3, S3a, etc. Cans which include an X, i.e., SX3p and others were produced for export. The 5-quart and 4-quart cans also carried a code but they were different than the codes carried by the 1-quarts. Other cans, such as 1-gallon square cans, 2-gallon square cans, even small Handy oil and lighter fluid cans also received codes.

Esso changed from 5-quart to 4-quart cans via an announcement in September, 1963, because about two-thirds of the cars on the highways at that time required only 4-quarts to fill their crankcases. The new 4-quart containers had the same diameter as the 5-quarts. They were just shorter and were made of metal. Most of the 1-quart cans at that time were fiber. It is also important to note here that only Uniflo and Esso Extras were produced in the 4-quart cans. I do not believe that Esso Motor Oil was ever produced in any factory-sealed round cans, other than the 1-quart size, after 1960.

1964

Although Esso Standard Oil Company had experimented with plastic motor oil cans as early as 1945, none were actually test marketed until 1964. Plastic was not deemed economical against steel in 1945, but because of a new process for making polyethylene developed by Enjay Chemical (Esso's sister chemical company), it was felt that it would be economical in 1964. The cans were plastic sides and bottom with metal tops. They were test marketed in Louisiana, Arkansas, and Tennessee. Only Esso Motor Oil in a red plastic can was test marketed. Reaction was favorable from both dealers and customers. In 1965, therefore, Esso expanded its variety of cans and started test marketing to about one hundred fifty service stations in the Baltimore, Maryland area. Four grades were tested: Uniflo in a gold can, Esso Extra in a blue can, Esso Motor Oil in a red can, and Essolube Motor Oil (a non-detergent motor oil) in white plastic cans with metal tops. The cans were solid color polyethylene with no body imprinting. Brand identification and other product information was imprinted on the tops of the cans. The experiment was not successful, and plastic cans were discontinued. However, plastic Esso Uniflo cans of the can code S1r do exist because I have one in my collection (Fig. 27), and plastic Enco Uniflo cans with code N1n exist because I have one of those as well (Fig. 28).

Figure 27

Figure 28

November, 1965

Humble Oil and Refining Company adopted a new identification system at this time by increasing the width of its oval around the names Esso, Enco, and Humble. The new oval was referred to as the "wide band" oval. On 1-quart cans, the size was increased from 1/8" to 3/16". Therefore, if you have a wide band oval can, you know it was produced after 1965.

1967

Esso introduced its first Uniflo 10w-40 Motor Oil, and new cans were produced. The can was solid gold in color. Uniflo was also available in 5w-30. As was customary at the same time, Esso Extra and Esso Motor Oils were improved and also sported new can designs. Between 1967 and 1973 (Exxon Company, U.S.A. was adopted on January 1, 1973) cans continued to undergo slight design changes. Primarily, Esso moved to eliminate a third color in their cans. They become two colors only: Esso Extra and Esso were silver and blue, and Uniflo was gold and blue (Fig. 29). Figure 29 shows what I believe to be the last cans produced under the Esso brand. The codes are Uniflo, S1s, Esso Extra, S2s and Esso Motor Oil, S3q.

I welcome comments from anyone who would like to add to or differ on anything contained in this story. Please contact me at (804) 272-8801.

Figure 29

Cans

Radiator Rust Preventive.
Size: 1-pint
Circa: 1950s
Value: $5-$10

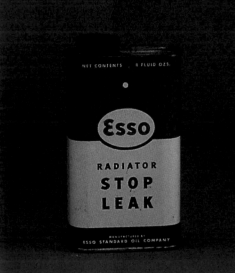

Radiator Stop Leak.
Size: 1-pint
Circa: 1950s
Value: $5-$10

Spot Remover.
Size: 1-pint
Circa: 1950s
Value: $5-$10

Koto Upper Motor Lube.
Size: 1-pint
Circa: 1940s-1950s
Value: $8-$15

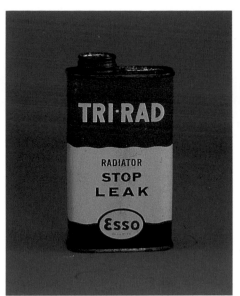

Tri-Rad Radiator Stop Leak.
Size: 1-pint
Circa: 1940s
Value: $8-$15

Trim Auto Polish.
Size: 1-pint
Circa: 1940s
Value: $8-$15

Koto Upper Motor Lube.
Size: 1-quart
Circa: 1940s-1950s
Value: $10-$20

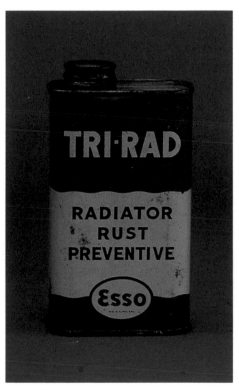

Tri-Rad Radiator Rust Preventive.
Size: 1-pint
Circa: 1940s
Value: $8-$15

Tri-Rad Radiator Stop Leak.
Size: 1-pint
Circa: 1930s
Value: $15-$20

Trim Auto Polish.
Size: 1-pint
Circa: 1930s Value: $15-$20

Trim Auto Polish.
Size: 2-ounce
Circa: 1920s Value: $15-$20

Esso Top Lube.
Size: 8-ounce
Circa: 1950s Value: $5-$10

Koto Upper Motor Lube bottle. Products were
packaged in bottles during World War II instead of
metal cans because of the restriction on the use of
metal for anything other than war materials.
Size: 1-quart
Circa: 1940s
Value: $25-$35

Esso Upper Motor Lube bottle.
Size: 1-pint
Circa: 1940s
Value: $25-$35

Tri-Rad Radiator Rust Preventive.
Size: 1-pint
Circa: 1940s
Value: $25-$35

Extane Spot Remover.
Size: 8-ounce
Circa: 1938-1942
Value: $25-$30

Uniflo Winter Motor Oil.
Circa: 1934
Value: 1-quart $75-$150; 5-quart $100-$200

Essolube Motor Oil.
Circa: 1939
Value: 1-quart $15-$25; 5-quart $25-$35

Esso Motor Oil (Unexcelled).
Circa: December, 1939
Value: 1-quart $25-$30; 5-quart $100-$150

How to Read Can Codes Found on Esso, Enco, and Humble Containers

On January 1, 1960, Esso Standard Oil Company, Carter, Pate, Oklahoma, and Humble Oil and Refining Company of Texas merged to form Humble Oil and Refining Company, Incorporated in Delaware. Everything had to be redesigned, not the least of which included the many containers used to transport the company's products to their customers. The old Carter, Pate, Oklahoma, and Humble organizations consolidated and became known as Enco, while Esso continued to market in the states they had marketed in prior to the consolidation. The state of Ohio would not allow either brand in their state, consequently Humble was used.

By 1962 these companies began to code their small containers. By looking at the code alone you cannot determine when the can was manufactured. However, by knowing other things about the can design you can approximate its age. For example, Esso, Enco, and Humble changed the width of the oval that surrounds the brand name in 1965. Therefore, if you have a can with a "thin band oval" you know it was manufactured sometime during the three years between 1962-1965. All cans after 1965 to 1972 inclusive carry the "wide band oval."

For those of us who consider ourselves advanced oil company can collectors, it is much easier to collect by code when dealing with this company's cans than it is to try and remember which design or color we have back home. When I attend a show or flea market, I carry my code sheets with me which contain my whole inventory of coded cans. Sometimes I make notes to myself about the condition of my cans because I might want to upgrade a particular one. In this way, I am actually using it as a checklist. Since this list contains only those cans in my collection that are coded, I still have to remember my uncoded ones as I did before. However, when it comes to Esso, Enco, and Humble, there are far more cans that contain a code than ones which do not.

Each time there was a change in design or material from which the can was made, a new letter was assigned. For example, Esso Uniflo Motor Oil 1-quart cans were assigned the beginning code of S1. When the first change was made, it was designated S1a then S1b, etc.

On the next page is a list of beginning codes that appear on different product containers.

1-Quart Round Motor Oil Cans

Symbol	Brand
S1	Esso Uniflo Motor Oil
N1	Enco Uniflo Motor Oil
H1	Humble Uniflo Motor Oil
S2	Esso Extra Motor Oil
N2	Enco Extra Motor Oil
H2	Humble Extra Motor Oil
S3	Esso Motor Oil
N3	Enco Motor Oil
H3	Humble Motor Oil
S4	Essolube HDX
N4	Encolube HDX
H4	Humblelube HDX

1-Quart Round Cans

Symbol	Brand
S5	Esso Automatic Transmission Fluid
N5	Enco Automatic Transmission Fluid
H5	Humble Automatic Transmission Fluid
S11	Essolube Motor Oil
N11	Encolube Motor Oil
H11	Humblelube Motor Oil
A9	Actol Motor Oil

4-Quart Round Cans

Symbol	Brand
S25	Esso Aviation Oil
N25	Enco Aviation Oil
S26	Esso Aviation Oil E
N26	Enco Aviation Oil E
S27	Esso Uniflo Motor Oil
N27	Enco Uniflo Motor Oil
S28	Esso Extra Motor Oil
N28	Enco Extra Motor Oil

5-Quart Round Motor Oil Cans

Symbol	Brand
S21	Esso Uniflo Motor Oil
N21	Enco Uniflo Motor Oil
H21	Humble Uniflo Motor Oil

Note: By 1963, 5-quart motor oil cans were replaced by the 4-quart variety. In an announcement made in December 1966, the S21 and N21 codes were assigned to Esso and Enco Turbo Oil 2380.

Esso Extra Motor Oil.
Circa: 1965
Value: 1-quart $10-$15; 4-quart $15-$25

Esso Uniflo Motor Oil.
Circa: 1967-1973
Value: 1-quart $15-$25; 4-quart $25-$35

4-Ounce Rectangular Metal Cans

Symbol	Brand
S100	Esso Handy Oil
N100	Enco Handy Oil
H100	Humble Handy Oil
S101	Esso Lighter Fluid
N101	Enco Lighter Fluid
H101	Humble Lighter Fluid

2-US Gallon Rectangular Oil Cans

Symbol	Brand
A200	Actol Motor Oil

Esso Aviation Oil. In 1938, Esso sold its one third share of its partnership in the Stanavo corporation, which had been formed in 1929 between the Standard Oil Company of California, Standard Oil Company of Indiana, and Standard Oil Company of New Jersey, to the remaining two companies. Esso wanted to market its own brand of Avgas and Aviation Oil. These are believed to be the first Aviation Oil cans used.
Size: 1-quart, 4-quart
Circa: 1938
Value: No Estimate

Esso Aviation Oil.
Size: 1-quart, 4-quart
Circa: 1945
Value: $100-$150, $200-$300

Various Esso Aviation Oil cans.
Size: 1-quart
Circa: 1950-1973
Value: $10-$25

Esso Aviation Oil.
Size: 4-quart
Circa: 1950s
Value: $40-$60

Univis Low
Temperature
Hydraulic Oil.
Size: 1-quart
Circa: 1936
Value: $20-$30

Various Esso Aviation Turbo Oil cans (synthetic oil). I am not aware of Turbo Oil being packaged in cans larger than 1-quart.
Size: 1-quart
Circa: 1959-1971
Value: $10-$75

Plastic Uniflo Motor Oil can.
Size: 1-quart
Circa: 1966
Value: $25-$35

Essolube HDX Motor Oil.
Size: 1-quart
Circa: 1965-1967
Value: $10-$15

Esso Extra and Esso Uniflo Motor Oil cans. In the mid-1950s, Esso decided to experiment with an all aluminum can and also a new can configuration. This was speculated to be an attempt to package more cans than usual in a container for export purposes. The experiment was abandoned shortly after it began. Although the author is unaware of the existence of an Esso Motor Oil can in addition to the ones mentioned above, it probably does exist.
Size: 1-quart
Circa: 1955
Value: $50-$75

Various Essolube Motor Oil cans.
Size: 1-quart
Circa: 1953-1967
Value: $10-$30

Various Esso Motor Oil cans.
Size: 1-quart
Circa: 1960-1966
Value: $10-$15

Alert Motor Oil. This was a low priced self-service gasoline company owned by Humble Oil and Refining Company.
Size: 1-quart
Circa: 1970
Value: $30-$50

Esso Marine Oil.
Size: 1-quart
Circa: 1950s
Value: $10-$20

Tri-Rad Anti Freeze.
Size: 1-quart
Circa: 1950s
Value: $15-$30

Actol Motor Oil cans.
Size: 1-quart
Circa: 1956-1965
Value: $15-$30

Esso Aquaglide Outboard Motor Oil.
Size: 1-pint
Circa: 1950s-1960s
Value: $10-$20

Esso Aquaglide
Outboard Motor Oil.
Size: 1-quart
Circa: 1960-1965
Value: $20-$30

Esso Aquaglide Outboard Motor Oil (plastic bottles).
Size: 1-quart
Circa: 1960s
Value: $5-$10

Assortment of Esso
Outboard lubricants.
The two grease tubes
at lower right are from
the mid '50s and the
others are from the
'60s.
Circa: 1950s-1960s
Value: $10-$25 each

Esso Aquaglide
Outboard Motor Oil.
The one on the right
was the first to appear.
It has a label on it that
says "NEW."
Size: 1-quart
Circa: 1959-1961
Value: $10-$20 each

Essoleum Grease cans. Note all three Standard Oil companies are present at the bottom of the can making them 1930s vintage.
Size: 5-pounds
Circa: 1930s
Value: $30-$50

Essoleum 1-Pound can wooden shipping box.
Circa: 1930s
Value: $50-$70

Estan Cup Grease. This can is identical to the Essoleum grease cans, including the three Standard Oil Companies shown at the bottom edge. It was apparently packaged like this to be marketed in the states not assigned to SONJ by the U S Supreme Court decision in 1911.
Size: 5-pounds
Circa: 1930s
Value: $30-$50

Essoleum Grease can. Note that Standard Oil Company of Louisiana has been omitted from the bottom edge of the can. This was done in 1945. Please see the history of the round factory filled cans which is described at the beginning of this chapter for more details.
Size: 1-pound
Circa: 1945
Value: $20-$25

Tri-Rad Anti-Freeze.
Size: 1-gallon
Circa: 1940s
Value: $20-$40

Essoleum Grease tubes.
Size: 2.5" diameter x 8" length (1-pound)
Circa: 1930s
Value: $25-$35 each

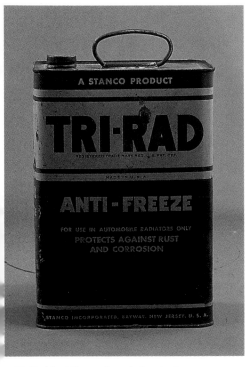

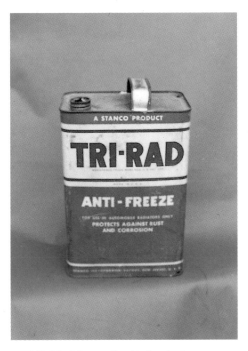

Tri-Rad Anti-Freeze (wire bail variety).
Size: 1-gallon
Circa: 1930s
Value: $25-$45

Tri-Rad Anti-Freeze (fixed bail variety).
Size: 1-gallon
Circa: 1930s
Value: $25-$45

Esso Extra Motor Oil. These cans were used for
export to other countries. However, as always,
some were sold in the United States.
Size: 1-gallon
Circa: 1960s
Value: $25-35 each

Esso Uniflo Motor Oil.
Size: 4-quart
Circa: Late 1960s
Value: $15-$25

Uniflo Motor Oil. This design was sold to the Skelly Oil Company for distribution in the western states.
Size: 5-quart
Circa: 1935
Value: $25-$35

Esso Anti-Freeze concentrated methanol type. This can also comes in a 1-quart variety.
Size: 4-quart
Circa: 1950s
Value: $20-$30

Esso Anti-Freeze alcohol-type. This can also came in a 1-quart variety.
Size: 4-quart
Circa: 1940s-1950s
Value: $20-$30

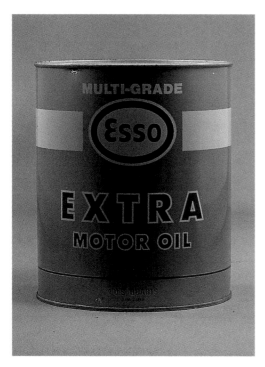

Esso Extra Motor Oil Multi-Grade.
Size: 4-quart
Circa: 1966
Value: $10-$20

Esso Extra Motor Oil.
Size: 4-quart
Circa: Late 1960s
Value: $10-$20

Esso Uniflo Motor Oil.
Size: 4-quart
Circa: Late 1960s
Value: $15-$25

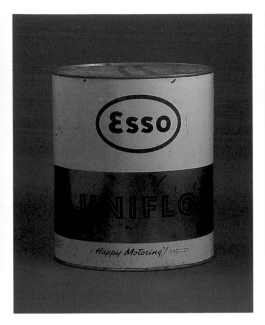

Esso Uniflo Motor Oil.
Size: 4-quart
Circa: 1963
Value: $15-$25

Esso Extra Motor Oil Multi-Grade.
Size: 4-quart
Circa: 1971
Value: $10-$15

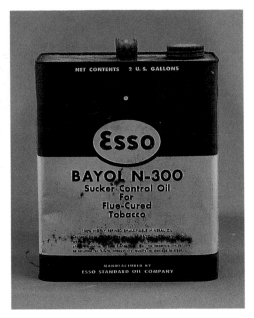

Bayol N-300. This product was used as a sucker control oil for the flue-cured tobacco industry.
Size: 2-gallon
Circa: 1950s
Value: $20-$30

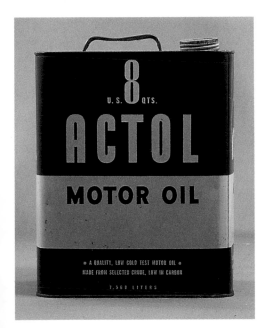

Actol Motor Oil was a non-detergent low priced motor oil for older cars and trucks. The product was also available in 1-quart cans.
Size: 2-gallon
Circa: 1950s
Value: $20-$30

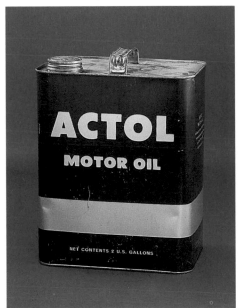

Actol Motor Oil (blue).
Size: 2-gallon
Circa: 1960s
Value: $20-$30

Actol Motor Oil (red). This is a very difficult can to find. I have only seen two.
Size: 2-gallon
Circa: 1960s
Value: $40-$50

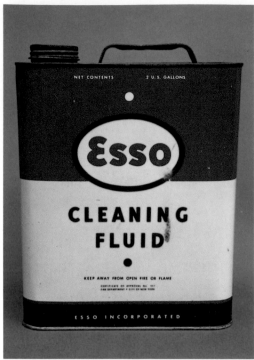

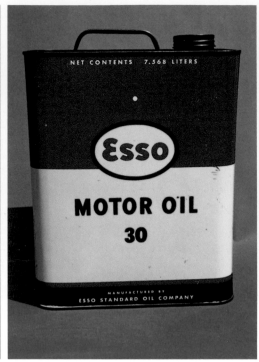

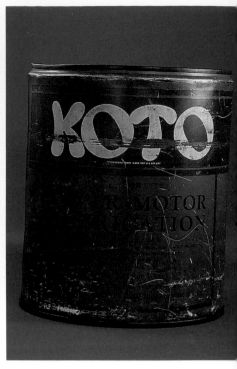

Esso Cleaning Fluid.
Size: 2-gallon
Circa: 1950s
Value: $20-$30

Esso Motor Oil.
Size: 2-gallon
Circa: 1950s
Value: $20-$30

Koto Upper Motor Lubricant.
Size: 5-gallon
Circa: 1930s
Value: $30-$50

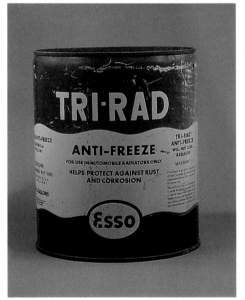

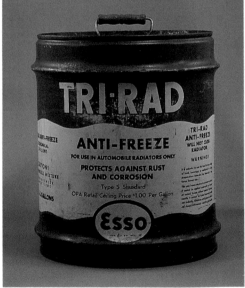

Koto Upper Motor Lubricant.
Size: 5-gallon
Circa: 1942
Value: $25-$35

Tri-Rad Anti-Freeze.
Size: 5-gallon
Circa: 1940
Value: $35-$45

Tri-Rad Anti-Freeze. This can has Government
World War II pricing on the side.
Size: 5-gallon
Circa: 1943
Value: $30-$50

Esso Leather Oil. The cans that have the product printed on the side when the can was made are more valuable than the ones that had the product name stenciled on the side at the warehouse.
Size: 5-gallon
Circa: 1939-1942
Value: $35-$50

Esso Varsol No.1.
Size: 5-gallon
Circa: 1950-1953
Value: $25-$35

Essolube Motor Oil.
Size: 5-gallon
Circa: 1945-1948
Value: $25-$50

Essoleum Expee Compound. This was a gear oil sold by the pound rather than by the gallon.
Size: 35-pounds (5-gallon)
Circa: 1930s
Value: $30-$60

Essoleum Expee Compound.
Size: 25-pounds
Circa: 1930s
Value: $25-$40

Nu-Trim Car Wax.
Circa: 1930s
Value: $15-$30

Nu-Trim Car Wax.
Circa: 1939-1943
Value: $10-$20

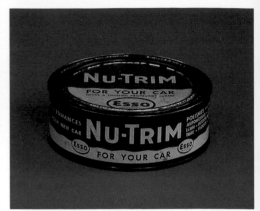

Nu-Trim Car Wax.
Circa: 1938-1941
Value: $15-$30

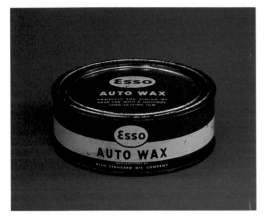

Esso Auto Wax.
Circa: 1950
Value: $15-$25

Esso Tank Anti-Rust. This product was introduced in 1953. It was a free service performed by the Esso truck driver when he came to fill your heating oil tank and provided up to three years of protection against the corrosive action of water. It settled to the bottom of the tank where the water is found and began its protective action there.
Size: 4-ounce
Circa: 1953-1960s
Value: $15-$25

Essoleum Chassis Lubricant H.
Size: 120-pounds
Circa: 1930s
Value: $50-$75

Esso Handy Oil. This is a very difficult can to find. It was the fifth in the series since its introduction in the early 1920s.
Size: 4-ounce
Circa: 1930s
Value: No Estimate

Esso Handy Oil.
Size: 1-ounce
Circa: 1938-1942
Value: $25-$55

Esso Handy Oil.
Size: 4-ounce
Circa: 1938-1942
Value: $35-$65

Esso Handy Oil (bottle). Because of the war restrictions on the use of metal for packaging petroleum products, products had to be packaged in glass bottles.
Size: 3-ounce
Circa: 1943-1945
Value: $25-$35

Esso Handy Oil.
Size: 4-ounce
Circa: 1946-1950
Value: $30-$50

Esso Handy Oil.
Size: 3-ounce
Circa: 1950s
Value: $15-$25

Esso Handy Oil. This was the first and only time Esso marketed Handy Oil in three grades at the same time.
Size: 3-ounce
Circa: 1951-1954
Value: $25-$35 each

Esso Handy Oil.
Size: 4-ounce
Circa: 1950s
Value: $15-$25

Esso Handy Oil. Happy the oil drop figure appeared in the United States in February of 1959 and this is the first can he appeared on. The yellow plastic figure of Happy is not USA but is very interesting nevertheless.
Size: 4-ounce
Circa: 1959
Value: $15-$25 (Plastic Happy $30-$75)

Esso Handy Oil. This is another variety of the yellow plastic figure of Happy.
Size: 4-ounce
Circa: 1960s
Value: $30-$75

Esso Handy Oil. These four cans are basically the same design except for oval sizes. The one on the right is a darker color and the two on the right are the same vintage. The small oval can was next and the can on the far left was last.
Size: 4-ounce
Circa: 1960-1967
Value: $10-$20

Opposite page:
Bottom left: Esso Lighter Fluid.
Size: 4-ounce
Circa: 1946-1950s
Value: $25-$40

Bottom center: Esso Lighter Fluid.
Size: 4-ounce
Circa: 1950s
Value: $20-$30

Esso Rust-Ban 392.
Size: 4-ounce
Circa: 1960s
Value: $10-$20

Bottom right: Esso Lighter Fluid.
Size: 4-ounce
Circa: 1960s
Value: $10-$20

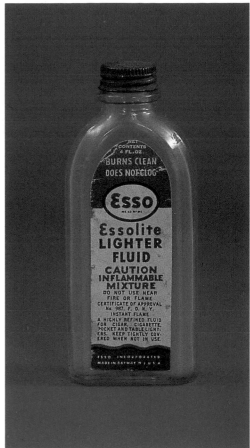

Esso Aviation Instrument oil. This is a difficult can to find.
Size: 4-ounce
Circa: 1940s
Value: No Estimate

Essolite Lighter Fluid.
Size: 4-ounce
Circa: April, 1938
Value: $30-$60

Essolite Lighter Fluid. This was a World War II product marketed in the familiar glass bottle.
Size: 4-ounce
Circa: 1943-1945
Value: $40-$65

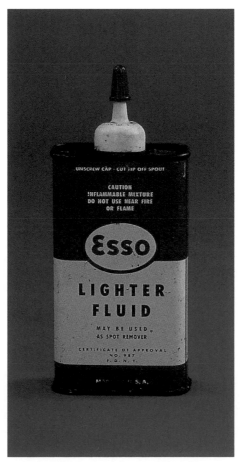

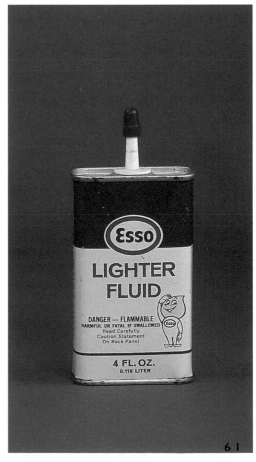

Esso Lighter Fluid. The can on the left is prior to 1965. In that year Esso increased the width of their oval. The can on the right is after 1965.
Size: 4-ounce
Circa: 1960s
Value: $10-$20

Esso Lighter Fluid. This was the last Esso Lighter Fluid can design before going to Exxon.
Size: 4-ounce
Circa: 1960s-1972
Value: $10-$20

Esso Lubricating Grease.
Size: 1-pound
Circa: 1960s
Value: $$15-$25

Parmo Petrolatum. This is a food grade grease. It was used to lubricate machinery where incidental contact with food products was possible.
Size: 1-pound
Circa: 1930s
Value: No Estimate

Esso script pump globe. When this globe was introduced in 1926 it was for the premium grade gasoline.
Circa: 1926
Value: 15" $450-$800; 16.5" $500-$1,000

New Esso decaled pump globe. New Esso Extra gasoline was introduced and became the premium grade in 1939. Until then, Esso had been the premium grade and Essolene the regular grade. Esso dropped down and became the regular grade replacing Essolene. "New Esso" decals were placed over the Essolene lenses until the new Esso lenses were installed.
Circa: 1939
Value: 15" $350-$450; 16.5" $400-$500

Bottom left: Esso Aviation globe.
Circa: 1950s
Glass Body: 13.5"
Value: $600-$800
Metal Body: 15" and 16.5"
Value: $800-$1,200 each

Bottom right: Esso Extra neon lighted pump globe. This is an 18" internally lighted globe. However, There are three other sizes of this same globe design.
Circa: 1939-1952
Value: 13.5" $300-$500; 15" $350-$500; 16.5" $450-$650; 18" No Listing

Acto pump globe. This was a sub-regular grade gasoline.
Circa: 1933-1939
Value: 15" $350-$450; 16.5" $450-$550

Left: National A-1 pump with Esso Extra glass inserts and pump globe. Right: National B-1 pump clock face with Esso glass inserts and Essolene pump globe.
Type: Electric
Circa: 1932
Value: Left $800-$1,000; Right $1,000-$1,200

Tokheim Model 36B with Esso glass inserts.
Type: Electric
Circa: 1938
Value: $1,000-$1,200

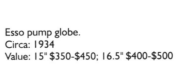

Esso pump globe.
Circa: 1934
Value: 15" $350-$450; 16.5" $400-$500

Wayne showcase pump with Esso pump globe.
Type: Electric
Circa: 1930s
Value: $1,500-$2,000

National A38 pump with Esso glass inserts
and pump globe.
Type Electric
Circa: 1936
Value: $800-$1,000

Gilbert & Barker T-86 with Esso glass inserts.
Type: Electric
Circa: 1938
Value: $1,000-$1,200

Essolene pump globe.
Circa: 1934
Value: 15" $450-$550; 16.5" $500-$600

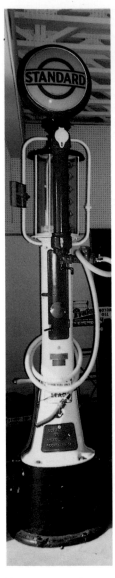

Fry gas pump with
Standard pump globe.
Type: 5-gallon Visible
Pump
Circa: 1920s-1940s
Value: $1,000-$2,000

Gilbert & Barker T-176 pump with
Essolene pump globe.
Type: 10-gallon Visible Pump
Circa: 1925-1950s
Value: $1,000-$2,000

Gilbert & Barker T-65
pump with Essolene pump
globe.
Type: 5-gallon Blind Pump
Circa: 1921
Value: $1,000-$1,500

Tokheim Model-34 display
pump with Essolene pump
globe.
Type: Electric
Circa: 1935
Value: $1,500-$2,000

Tokheim Model-34 pump
with Esso Extra pump globe.
Type: Electric
Circa: 1934
Value: $800-$1,000

Golden Esso Extra pump globe.
This was a super premium
gasoline.
Circa: 1956-1963
Value: No Estimate

Esso Extra with red underline.
Circa: 1952-1962
Value: 15" $350-$450; 16.5" $400-$500

Esso Plus pump globe. This was a middle grade gasoline.
Circa: 1963-1972
Value: 13.5" $200-$300

Esso Diesel pump globe.
Circa: 1940-1962
Value: 15" $350-$500

Esso Kerosene pump globe
Circa: 1940-1962
Value: 15" $300-$400; 16.5" $450-$550

Signs

Essomarine Oils & Greases. One-sided porcelain.
Size: 24" x 16"
Circa: 1930s
Value: $400-$1,000

Esso Credit Cards Honored. "Buy at the Esso Sign." Two-sided porcelain.
Size: 18" x 14"
Circa: 1930s
Value: $250-$350

Esso Credit Cards Honored. This sign does not have the words "Buy at the" as the previous sign had. Two-sided porcelain.
Size: 18" x 14"
Circa: 1940s
Value: $250-$400

Esso Credit Cards Honored. Two-sided porcelain.
Size: 18" x 14"
Circa: 1950-1970
Value: $200-$275

Esso Motor Oil rack sign. Two-sided porcelain.
Size: 18" x 10"
Circa: 1935-1939
Value: $150-$250

Essoleum Lubricants From Sealed Cartridges. One-sided enamel.
Size: 13" x 7"
Circa: 1930s
Value: $50-$100

Winged Esso Oval Aviation. Plastic.
Size: 60" x 24"
Circa: 1950s
Value: $150-$200

Esso Aviation Gasoline. One-sided "pit" sign, enamel.
Size: 20" x 5.5"
Circa: 1940s
Value: $200-$300

Essolube Motor Oil rack sign, 25 cents. Two-sided enamel.
Size: 18" x 10"
Circa: 1937
Value: $75-$125

Essolube Motor Oil rack sign. Two-sided enamel.
Size: 18" x 10"
Circa: 1937
Value: $75-$125

Essolube Motor Oil rack sign. Two-sided enamel.
Size: 17.5" x 10.75"
Circa: 1947
Value: $75-$125

Essolube Motor Oil rack sign. Two-sided enamel.
Size: 14" x 10"
Circa: 1942
Value: $100-$150

Esso Extra Motor Oil rack sign. One-sided porcelain.
Size: 17.5" x 10.75"
Circa: 1950
Value: $175-$225

Esso Uniflo Motor Oil rack sign. One-sided enamel.
Size: 17.5" x 10.5"
Circa: 1959
Value: $75-$125

Esso Oil Change rack sign. One-sided enamel.
Size: 17.5" x 10.5"
Circa: 1960
Value: $50-$75

Esso Extra Motor Oil rack sign. Two-sided enamel. This sign is also
available in a one-sided variety.
Size: 17.5" x 10.5" (Both)
Circa: 1950 (Both)
Value: One-sided $50-$75; Two-sided $75-$125

Esso Motor Oil rack sign. Two-sided enamel. This sign is also available with
"Something Extra For Your Money / Esso Extra Motor Oil" on the opposite
side.
Size: 17.5" x 10.5" (Both)
Circa: 1947 (Both)
Value: Same on both sides $75-$125; Different on both sides $100-$175

Humble & Esso Uniflo "Finest Protection Money Can Buy." One-sided enamel.
Size: 17.5" x 10.5"
Circa: 1968
Value: $25-$75

Esso Motor Oil "Worlds Finest Lubricant" rack sign.
Size: 20.5" x 10"
Circa: 1930s
Value: $125-$175

Esso Extra Motor Oil rack sign. Two-sided porcelain. This sign was
only used in Texas.
Size: 21.5" x 11"
Circa: 1950s
Value: $75-$125

HIGHEST VISCOSITY INDEX

Uniflo
MOTOR OIL

LOWEST CONSUMPTION

Uniflo Motor Oil rack sign. Two-sided porcelain.
Size: 15.5" x 13"
Circa: 1930s
Value: $100-$250

Uniflo Motor Oil. One-sided enamel. This sign has a banner across the company name so the same sign could be used in Esso territory as well as other parts of the country where Esso was not allowed to market.
Size: 20" x 15.5"
Circa: 1968
Value: $50-$75

Esso Motor Oil Lowest Consumption Easiest Starting. Two-sided enamel.
Size: 17.5" x 10.5
Circa: 1937
Value: $100-$150

Essotane Authorized Dealer sign. One-sided porcelain.
Size: 22" x 12.5"
Circa: 1940s
Value: $150-$250

Esso Service

Esso Service. One-sided porcelain sign. This sign was mounted on top of truck cabs advertising the truck as an Esso vehicle carrying fuel. It also came in a large size, which would have been mounted on a fence next to Esso Service Stations.
Size: Truck Sign 43" x 6"; Service Station Sign 102" x 14"
Value: $150-$200; $100-$150
Circa: 1940s

Esso script round porcelain. Reverse has the Standard Bar & Circle logo. This sign comes in two sizes.
Size: 42"; 36"
Value: $160-$225; $200-$300
Circa: 1926

Essolube Motor Oil. One-sided porcelain wall sign.
Size: 36" x 17.5"
Circa: 1940s
Value: $100-$200

Esso aluminum and plastic oval. This sign came out of the district office in Columbia, South Carolina, when the name changed to Exxon.
Size: 27" x 19"
Circa: 1972
Value: No Estimate

Esso two-sided porcelain sign.
Size: 36" x 17.5"
Circa: 1960s
Value: $150-$250

Esso script free-standing driveway sign. Two-sided porcelain. This sign was only used in the New England states.
Size: 30" x 25.5"
Circa: 1926-1933
Value: $250-$350

Esso, The Giant Power
Fuel gasoline advertising
sign. One-sided enamel.
Size: 15" x 8.5"
Circa: 1929
Value: $100-$175

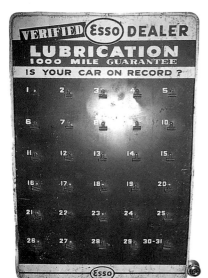

Esso Verified Lubrication customer
notification sign. When a customer
had his car serviced at a service
station the owner would estimate
when he should return for another
service visit. He would clip a
postcard on this board and on that
day of the month he would send
the customer a reminder.
Size: 44.5" x 30"
Circa: 1930s
Value: $100-$175

Esso Products for Your
Car and Home display
rack, porcelain.
Size: 44" x 24"
Circa: 1930s
Value: $175-$250

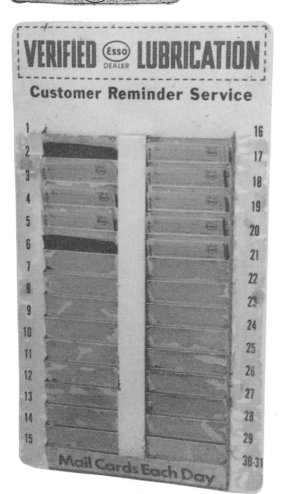

Bottom left: Esso
Verified Lubrication
customer notification
sign. This is another
variety of the
previous sign.
Size: 32.5" x 19"
Circa: 1940s
Value: $75-$150

Bottom right: Esso
Lubrication
Guarantee. This is
another variation of
the former two signs.
Notice that the word
"Verified" has been
eliminated, which
occurred in the
1950's
Size: 44.5" x 30"
Circa: 1950s
Value: $100-$175

Esso Heating Oils Authorized Dealer. Two-sided enamel with the words Esso Kerosene appearing on the reverse.
Size: 35" x 21"
Circa: 1950s
Value: $100-$175

Reverse of the Esso Heating Oils sign.

Esso Heating Oil. Two-sided porcelain sign.
Size: 35" x 21"
Circa: 1950s
Value: $200-$300

Sanitized Rest Rooms sign. Two-sided porcelain. This sign was displayed on the identification sign pole along with the Esso credit card sign at every service station.
Size: 24" x 18"
Circa: 1940s-1950s
Value: $100-$150

Esso plastic sign. This sign came in at least five sizes.
Size: 17" x 12"; 28" x 20"; 34" x 24"; 42" x 30"; 51" x 36"
Value: $100-$150; $50-$75; $60-$80; $60-$90; $75-$150
Circa: 1960s

Esso Oil Burners one-sided wall sign
Size: 35"x21"
Circa: 1950s-1960s
Value: $100-$175

Esso Aviation Oil pedestal sign. Two-sided enamel on metal.
Size: 24"
Circa: 1940s
Value: $500-$600 (higher with base)

Esso Aviation Products pedestal sign. Two-sided enamel on metal with a different message on the reverse.
Size: 24"
Circa: 1930s & 1940s
Value: $700-$800

Reverse of the Esso Aviation Products sign.

Esso Motor Oil Unexcelled with wooden frame. One-sided enamel.
Size: 72" x 36"
Circa: 1930s
Value: $200-$300

Base for the two-sided pedestal sign shown above.

Esso Verified Lubrication with wooden frame.
One-sided enamel.
Size: 72" x 36"
Circa: 1930s
Value: $200-$300

Esso Extra Motor Oil with wooden frame.
One-sided enamel.
Size: 72" x 36"
Circa: 1950s
Value: $200-$300

Esso Lubrication Service with wooden frame.
One-sided enamel.
Size: 72" x 36"
Circa: 1950s
Value: $200-$300

Esso Verified Lubrication. One-sided
porcelain.
Size: 32" x 8"
Circa: 1930s
Value: $150-$300

"Standard" Esso Dealer. Two-sided porcelain sign. In 1934, Standard Oil Company began to identify all of their service stations with this type of sign. It came in two sizes, major and minor. The size of the facility determined the kind of sign used. If the station was a dealer operation this is the sign they had. If it was a company owned station, the sign said "Standard" Esso Station, instead of Dealer. Since all company owned stations were large, there were no minor "Standard" Esso Station signs. In 1936, the company decided to do away with the Station part of the sign and make them all Dealer. Rather than change all the signs immediately, however, they decided to drill two holes on either side of word Station and bolt a porcelain sign over it that said Dealer.
Size: Major 88" x 60"; Minor 60" x 40"
Value: $100-$200; $250-$400
Circa: 1934-1948

Dealer porcelain re-identification sign. This is one of the porcelain signs that was used to cover the word Station on the major "Standard" Esso Station signs in 1936.
Size: 34" x 6.75"
Circa: 1936
Value: No Estimate

Esso Wide Band Oval Major ID sign.
Size: 88" x 60"
Circa: 1965-1973
Value: $75-$150

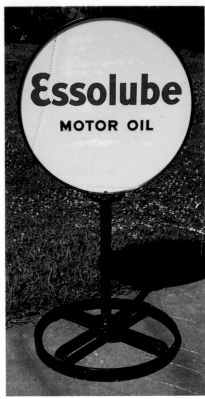

Tiger decal over Esso Wide Band Oval Major ID sign. In the 1960s, when Chevron purchased the Standard Oil Company of Kentucky (KYSO), Esso tried to raise the Esso sign in territory that had not been authorized in the 1911 Supreme Court's decision. Esso claimed that since they had supplied all the products that KYSO had marketed, meaning that KYSO had been a huge distributor of Esso products, they had earned the right to "fly their colors." The court didn't see it that way. Chevron filed suit and the court ordered Esso to re-identify their stations at once. Overnight Esso had to put decals of the Tiger over the Esso signs until they could put Enco signs up as permanent replacements.
Size: 88" x 60"
Circa: 1965
Value: $150-$200

Essolube pedestal two-sided porcelain sign.
Size: 24"
Circa: 1940s
Value: $100-$200

Esso island light insert. Internally lighted.
Size: 18.5" x 14"
Circa: 1960s
Value: $75-$150

Esso Outboard Motor Oil cardboard sign.
Size: 30" x 10"
Circa: 1960s
Value: $40-$50

Esso Rent-A-Car sign, framed and internally lighted.
Circa: 1960s
Value: $150-$200

Esso-Humble Distributor sign.
Size: 93" x 34"
Circa: 1960s-1970s
Value: $50-$100

Atlas Pole Sign with Esso oval Use Your Credit Card.
Size: 18" x 14"
Circa: 1950s
Value: $100-$150

Esso advertising poster.
Size: 30" x 14"
Circa: 1929
Value: $150-$200

Map Racks

Esso map rack, metal.
Size: 26.5" x 12"
Circa: 1938
Value: $150-$250

Esso map rack, wire.
Size: 20.5" x 4.5"
Circa: 1950s
Value: $75-$125

Esso map rack, metal.
Size: 23.5" x 13.5"
Circa: 1940s
Value: $150-$250

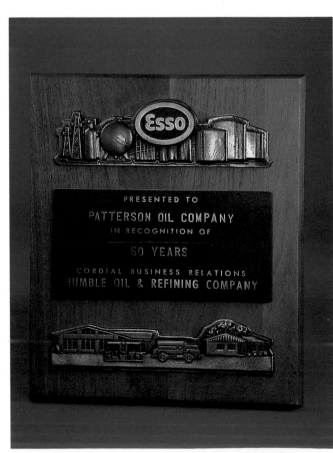

Esso Travel Center
map rack, metal and
plastic.
Size: 42" x 25.5"
Circa: 1960s
Value: $200-$250

Award Plaques

Inter-Fleet Safety
Award presented to
Standard Oil
Company of New
Jersey in 1932 by the
Richmond, Virginia
Safety Council.
Size: 21" x 16"
Value: No Estimate

Esso Customer Service
Award.
Size: 13" x 11"
Circa: 1960s
Value: $50-$70

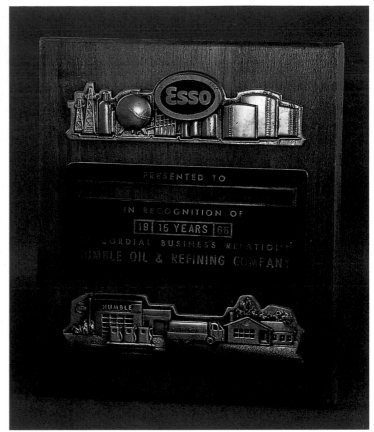

Esso Customer Service Award.
Size: 10.5" x 10"
Circa: 1960s
Value: $50-$60

Esso Customer Service Award.
Size: 13" x 10"
Circa: 1960s
Value: $50-$70

Esso Customer Service Award.
Size: 11" x 9"
Circa: 1954
Value: $75-$100

Esso Customer Service Award.
Size: 14" x 8"
Circa: 1958
Value: $75-$100

Esso Customer Service Award.
Size: 12" x 9"
Circa: 1939
Value: $150-$175

Esso Customer Service Award.
Size: 13" x 10"
Circa: 1959
Value: $75-$100

Locks and Miscellaneous

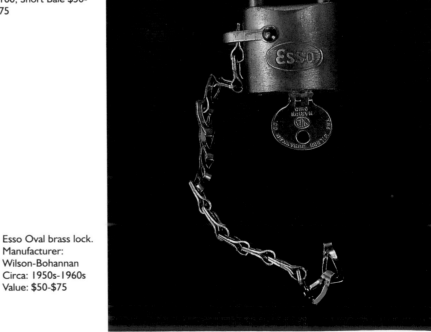

Esso brass locks.
Property of Esso
Standard Oil Co.
Manufacturer: Best
Circa: 1950s
Value: Long Bale $50-
$100; Short Bale $50-
$75

Esso Oval brass lock.
Manufacturer:
Wilson-Bohannan
Circa: 1950s-1960s
Value: $50-$75

Esso Oval brass lock.
Manufacturer: Wilson-Bohannan
Circa: 1950s-1960s
Value: $50-$75

Essotane wooden spoon customer giveaway.
Size: 10" x 2"
Circa: 1950s
Value: $25-$35

Esso Aviation windsock. This was an item used at airports to determine wind direction for planes landing and taking off. It symbolized to pilots that they could obtain Esso aviation products at this field.
Size: 8' 1" (length) x 2.5' (wide opening) x 1" (narrow opening)
Circa: 1960s
Value: $50-$60

Esso paint by Sherwin-Williams. Many different paint manufacturers mixed the paints used by Esso through the years.
Size: 1-quart
Circa: 1940s
Value: $15-$25

Esso gift set. Contains one Esso lighter fluid can and one Esso Handy Oil can plus a trip planning map of the United States.
Size: 8.25" x 5.25"
Circa: 1958
Value: $35

Banners

Esso script cloth banner.
Size: 6'6" x 3'
Circa: 1920s
Value: $200-$300

Esso station cloth banner.
Size: 5' x 3'
Circa: 1930s
Value: $75-$100

Aerotype Esso cloth banner.
Size: 6'8" x 35"
Circa: 1930s
Value: $150-$250

Essolene cloth banner.
Size: 79" x 36"
Circa: 1930s
Value: $175-$250

Esso Happy Motoring cloth banner. The "Happy Motoring!" motto was adopted by Esso in April, 1935.
Size: 137" x 55"
Circa: 1935
Value: $200-$300

Esso Care Saves Wear cloth banner. This was a popular saying during World War II. Esso was trying to encourage people to take care of their cars because you could not buy another one at that time and no one knew when you would be able to again.
Size: 8'9" x 2'10"
Circa: 1942-1945
Value: $100-$200

Esso Extra Gasoline cloth banner.
Size: 82" x 33"
Circa: 1940s
Value: $100-$200

Esso Extra Anti-Stalling Gasoline cloth banner.
Size: 79" x 34"
Circa: 1950s
Value: $100-$150

Esso Extra Gasoline with Vitane cloth banner.
Size: 60" x 39"
Circa: 1950s
Value: $75-$100

Esso Clean Rest Rooms cloth banner.
Size: 58" x 33"
Circa: 1950s
Value: $75-$100

Esso Extra Gasoline with D-Frost cloth banner.
Size: 82" x 36"
Circa: 1956
Value: $150-$200

Golden Esso Extra Gasoline cloth banner.
Size: 81" x 36"
Circa: 1956
Value: $175-$200

Esso Official Fueling Station Of The Glidden Tour. This is a tour that still continues today. It is a get-together of vintage cars for a multi-day tour of some part of the United States. Along the pre-planned route, gasoline stations are designated for fueling stops. This was a cloth banner that each Esso Service Station installed in 1957 to inform the car drivers that it was an official fueling station.
Size: 81" x 36"
Circa: 1957
Value: $75-$100

Esso Glidden Tour cloth banner. Each
car was given this ID banner with its
number imprinted.
Size: 16" x 16"
Circa: 1957
Value: $50-$75

Below: Esso World's First Choice, Happy the
Oil Drop cloth banner.
Size: 83" x 36"
Circa: 1959
Value: $100-$200

New Formula Esso Extra Gasoline cloth banner.
Size: 83" x 36"
Circa: 1960s
Value: $125-$200

Put a Tiger in Your Tank cloth banner.
Size: 84" x 42"
Circa: 1964
Value: $175-$210

ANTI-STALLING ESSO **EXTRA** GASOLINE

SAVES
TIME

SAVES
TEMPERS

SAVES
CARS

Anti-Stalling Esso Extra Gasoline cloth banner.
Size: 79" x 34"
Circa: 1960s
Value: $40-$60

EXXON
We're changing our name.

Exxon We're Changing Our Name cloth banner. On January 1, 1973 Esso officially changed their name to Exxon and employed the Tiger to help with the change.
Size: 70" x 42"
Circa: 1972
Value: $150-$250

Flit

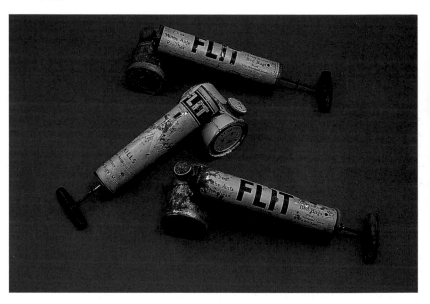

Flit insecticide sprayers. The sprayers were the first instruments used to dispense this product. Here they are shown by decade; notice the color change of the containers as time passed. These are from the beginning in the 1920s.
Circa: 1920s
Value: $75-$100

Flit was the brand name for a line of insecticides introduced in 1924 and sold to jobbers and retailers. These products reached the consumers through such retail outlets as drug, hardware, and general stores. Flit was also sold in service stations. This was a low volume product for Jersey Standard compared to the millions of gallons of fuels they sold. However, like other specialty products, Flit could be sold outside the nineteen states assigned by the 1911 Supreme Court decision and allowed the company to establish itself in other parts of the country. When we think of Flit, we naturally think of an atomized liquid that is expelled into the atmosphere to kill flies. While that's true, this brand name was also placed on other products that were not sprayed. Examples of these would be ant traps, lotion (applied to human skin), and powders with DDT added, to name a few. The origin of the name Flit is unknown but it is generally accepted that it stood for F-flies, L-lice, I-insects, T-ticks.

One of the most interesting sidelights about this product is the person who was hired to promote it. He was to become one of America's most celebrated illustrators and authors of children's books later in his career. His name was Theodor Seuss Geisel, better known to all of us as Dr. Seuss. Dr. Seuss worked for Jersey Standard from about 1928 to 1941. In an early interview he related that he had designed an ad campaign for insecticide and boiled it down to two major companies to present to. He flipped a coin to decide and Standard Oil Company of New Jersey won.

Today, because of lack of demand, Flit is no longer marketed.

Flit sprayers. Most of the sprayers are dated through the 1940s. The date is found under the Flit name near the end of the tube that attaches to the can or bottle that holds the liquid. The middle sprayer in this picture is actually dated on the end of the can facing you, 1932.
Circa: 1930s
Value: $50-$75

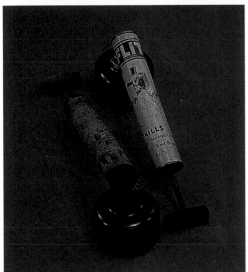

Flit sprayers. When World War II ended the company went back to producing metal sprayers. There are two sizes of the same sprayer pictured here, neither of which is dated, and a glass bowl type dated 1946.
Circa: Late 1940s
Value: $20-$30

Flit sprayers. During World War II, metal was an essential material and in such short supply that the use of it was restricted. Many companies had to package their products in glass bottles; these products included motor oil, handy oil, and lighter fluid to name just a few. Flit was no exception. The sprayer on the right still has the metal rod but notice that glass bowls have replaced the metal cans for both sprayers. The sprayer on the left has been fitted with a wooden rod (it was a little larger in diameter than the regular metal one) which represented the second transition that took place toward replacing metal in these sprayers.
Circa: 1940s
Value: $15-$25

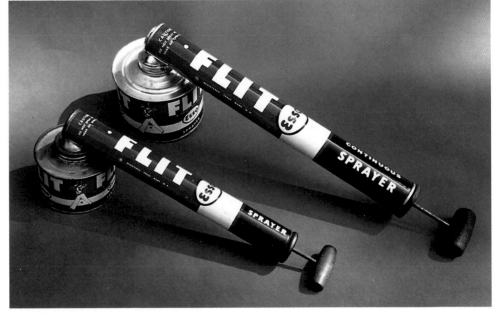

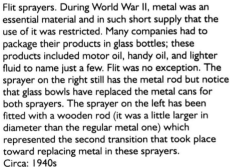

Flit sprayers. There are two sizes of the same design pictured here. Also, note a total color change to red, white, and blue. These were the last designs used for sprayers.
Circa: 1950s-1960s
Value: $20-$30

Flit sprayers. By the end of World War II, all metal had been completely eliminated from these sprayers. The bowl was glass, the attachment was plastic, the tube was cardboard, the rod was wooden, and the handle was wooden.
Circa: 1945
Value: $20-$30

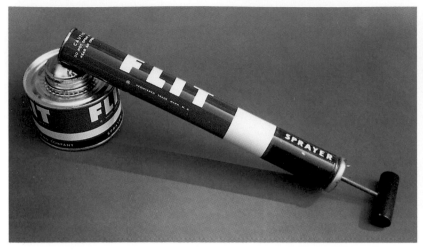

Flit sprayer. This sprayer does not have the name Esso on it anywhere. This was a sprayer design to be used legally outside the Esso marketing area.
Circa: 1950s-1960s
Value: $25-$35

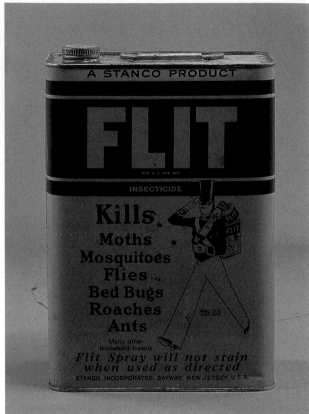

Flit can. The product was also available in other size containers.
Size: 1-gallon
Circa: 1930s
Value: $20-$30

Flit cans. The insecticide came in all size cans and would then be transferred to a sprayer for use.
Circa: 1920s
Value: $25-$50

Flit cans.
Circa: 1930s
Value: $15-$25

Flit can. This can reads "New Style Package Adopted 1928." I believe this means that the initial use of the Flit soldier started in 1928.
Size: 5-gallon
Circa: 1928
Value: $150-$300

Flit can.
Size: 5-gallon
Circa: 1930s
Value: $50-$75

Flit bottle. Here is another example of a wartime bottle.
Size: 1-pint
Circa: 1940s
Value: $25-$50

Flit can.
Size: 1-gallon
Circa: 1950s
Value: $20-$30

Flit cans. During the 1950s, Esso began adding other killing ingredients to the basic formula, such as DDT, Aromin, and Lindane. Note in this picture that a sprayer which screwed directly onto the cans was available. This was not the first design for this sprayer. A similar sprayer was available in the 1930s that screwed directly onto the cans as well.
Circa: 1950s
Value: $10-$20

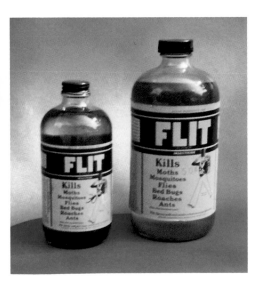

Flit bottles. Not only did the sprayer transition to a non-metal content during World War II, so did the cans. Here is an example of the bottles that were used.
Size: 1-pint; 1-quart
Circa: 1940s
Value: $25-$50

Flit powder. Products were also produced for other uses and in powder form.
Circa: 1930s
Value: $15-$25

Flit Bug Killer, round can.
Size: 4-ounce
Circa: 1950s
Value: $15-$20

Flit garden pump sprayers. This product came in two sizes, small and large as shown here, and was used for common garden pests.
Circa: 1940s
Value: $20-$30

Flit surface spray.
Size: 1-gallon
Circa: 1930s-1940s
Value: $25-$55

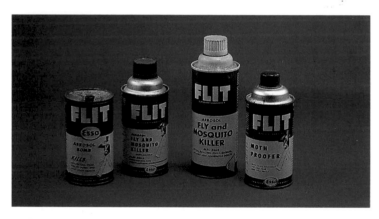

Flit aerosol cans.
Circa: 1950s
Value: $10-$20

Flit aerosol and pump cans.
Circa: 1950s
Value: $10-$20

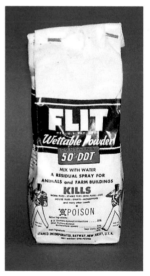

Flit wettable powder with 50 percent DDT. You mixed this product with water and sprayed it on animals and farm buildings.
Container: 1-pound bag
Circa: 1930s-1940s
Value: $30-$40

Flit household deodorant In a counter display
Circa: 1950s
Value: $60-$100

Flit ant traps in counter display.
Circa: 1950s
Value: $60-$100

Flit advertising.
Circa: 1930s
Value: $40-$75

Flit moth proofer aerosol in a counter display. Some of the Flit products came in counter display boxes packaged two to a case. This made them ready to sell complete with eye-catching advertising.
Circa: 1950s
Value: $60-$100

Flit advertising.
Circa: 1928
Value: $100-$200

Flit advertising. This is a wooden sign, no doubt created for a country store.
Size: 46" x 28"
Circa: 1950s
Value: $150-$250

Flit advertising. This was a novel way to advertise. I have seen other products take advantage of this level in their advertising as well.
Circa: 1950s
Value; $25-$35

Flit advertising. This is another wooden sign. However, this one is in the shape of the Flit soldier with the phrase made famous in the late 1930s and 1940s "Quick, Henry, the Flit."
Size: 72" x 42"
Circa: 1950s
Value: $200-$400

Flit product rack. These racks were used for store displays and were a way to display the product complete with advertising.
Size: 44" x 16.5"
Circa: 1950s
Value: $50-$150

Flit product rack, "Quick, Henry, the Flit."
Size: 44" x 16.5"
Circa: 1940s
Value: $50-$150

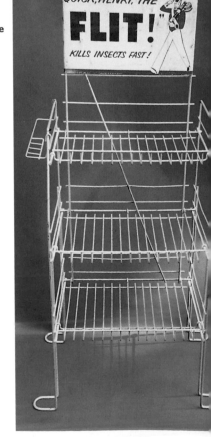

Flit advertising, various paper items.
Circa: 1940s
Value: $25-$75

Top left: Flit product rack, "Quick, Henry, the Flit."
Size: 44" x 16.5"
Circa: 1950s
Value: $50-$150

Top center: Flit product rack featuring aerosol ad.
Size: 44" x 16.5"
Circa: 1950s
Value: $50-$150

Thermometers

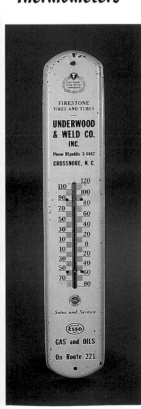

Esso thermometer.
Size: 3.25" x 17.5"
Circa: 1930s
Value: $75-$125

Esso with Atlas thermometer.
Size: 12" x 12"
Circa: 1940s-1950s
Value: $100-$150

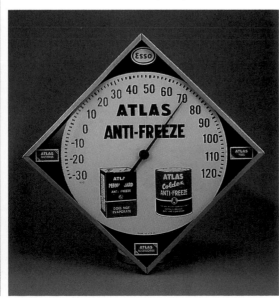

Esso Happy Oil Drop thermometer.
Size: 26.5" x 8.5"
Circa: 1960
Value: $150-$250

9 5

Uniform Patches

Essolube uniform patch.
Size: 10" x 5"
Circa: 1930s
Value: $10-$25

Winged Esso oval coverall patch.
Size: Large 13.5"x3" Small 5"x1.5"
Value: $30-$50; $20-$30
Circa: 1938

Happy Motoring World's Fair uniform patch. Service station attendants around New York during the 1939 and 1940 New York World's Fair wore this patch.
Size: 4.5" x 3.5"
Circa: 1939
Value: $75-$100

Esso script jacket patch.
Size: 8"
Circa: 1920s
Value: $50-$100

Esso uniform patches.
Circa: 1930s-1940s
Value: $10-$20

Esso uniform patches. Notice the patch with the wide band oval. The oval size was changed in 1965.
Circa: 1930s-1960s
Value: $10-$20

Esso uniform patches.
Circa: 1960s-1970s
Value: $10-$20

Try Golden. This patch was issued to announce the new Golden Esso Extra gasoline.
Size: 3.5" x 2"
Circa: 1956
Value: $20-$30

Esso safe driving uniform patch. The truck drivers who delivered the product to the service stations wore this patch.
Size: 4" x 3.5"
Circa: 1957
Value: $15-$30

Various Esso patches.
Circa: 1960s
Value: $20-$30

Esso safe driving uniform patch.
Size: 4.5" x 3"
Circa: 1960s
Value: $10-$20

Essotane uniform patch. As the patch indicates, Essotane was the name of the liquefied petroleum gas product.
Size: 3" x 4"
Circa: 1950s
Value: $15-$25

Esso Rent-A-Car uniform patch. Esso was in the rent-a-car business in the 1960s. This business ended about 1969.
Size: 3.5" x 2.25"
Circa: 1960s
Value: $15-$25

Esso Car Care Center, Car Wash, and Self Serve patches. The Esso Car Care Center concept was introduced about 1970. It was company owned, featured full service including mechanical work, and introduced self-serve gasoline service.
Sizes: 4"x 2.25"; 3" x 2.25"; 2" x 2.25"
Circa: 1970s
Value: $15-$25

Various Happy uniform patches. Happy the Oil Drop mascot was introduced in the United States in 1959 and remained until the Tiger was introduced in 1964.
Sizes: 5.75" x 3.75"; 4.5" x 4"; 3.5" x 2"
Circa: 1960s
Value: $15-$30

Esso Tours and Detours

Esso *Tours and Detours*. These are examples of some of the publications that continued until they ended in the 1950s.
Circa: 1930s-early 1940s
Value: $8-$10

In 1932, the General Drafting Company Inc. initiated an experiment in good will for the Standard Oil Company of New Jersey and some of its associated companies. Beginning with that year, six issues of three different editions of Esso *Tours and Detours* were published covering eleven states and the District of Columbia.

During the 1932 touring season over three million copies of Esso *Tours and Detours* were distributed to motorists from Standard service stations. The value of the new publication to the attendants of the sta-

tions must have been considerable, judging from the newspaper publicity and the many letters of appreciation received by the editors at General Drafting. This publication supplemented the service rendered to motorists by the "Standard" Touring Service which had been in service since the 1920s. *Tours and Detours* was published for Standard Oil Company of New Jersey, Standard Oil Company of Louisiana, Standard Oil Company of Pennsylvania, and Standard Oil Company of Kentucky. Later, the Colonial Esso division also received editions.

Esso *Tours and Detours*. Over the years the masthead changed many times. It was almost as though they "couldn't get it right."
Circa: late 1940s-1950s
Value: $8-$10

Colonial Esso *Tours and Detours* began in June 1934.
Circa: 1934-1940s
Value: $8-$10

The Esso Dealer began in 1926.
Circa: 1936
Value: $8-$10

Stock Certificates

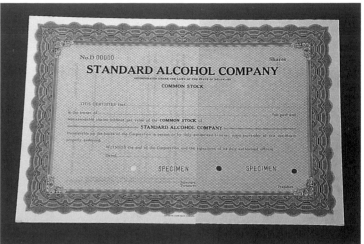

The Standard Alcohol Company stock certificate specimen. This became Esso Chemical Company in the 1930's.
Circa: 1920s
Value: No Estimate

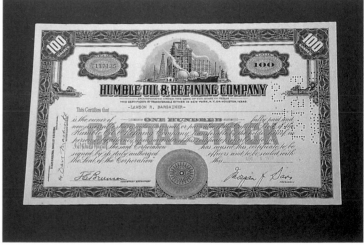

Humble Oil and Refining Company stock certificate specimen.
Circa: 1918
Value: No Estimate

Esso Incorporated stock certificate specimen.
Circa: 1930s
Value: No Estimate

Standard Oil Company of Pennsylvania stock certificate specimen.
Circa: 1930s
Value: No Estimate

Standard Oil Company of New Jersey stock certificate specimen
Circa: 1920s
Value: No Estimate

Standard Alcohol Company stock certificate multi-color specimens.
Circa: 1920s
Value: No Estimate

Lighters, Matches, Ashtrays

Esso lighter. This lighter is shaped like a shotgun shell. Script Esso appears on the firing pin end of the shell.
Circa: 1920s
Value: $50-$100

Esso lighter. This is the only item I have seen other than a map that has the stylized Esso logo on it.
Manufacturer: Beattie
Circa: 1937
Value: $50-$100

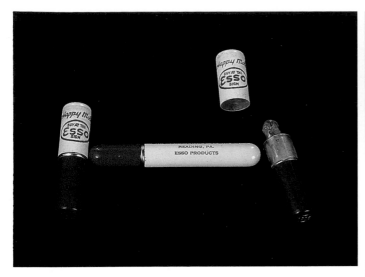

Esso lighters.
Circa: 1930s
Value: $15-$30

Esso lighters.
Manufacturer: Park
Circa: 1950s
Value: $35-$50

Esso lighters.
Manufacturer: Zippo
Circa: 1950s
Value: $35-$50

Esso lighters.
Manufacturer: Warco and Rolex
Circa: 1950s
Value: $35-$60

Esso lighter. This lighter has two wicks.
Manufacturer: Beacon Dub-I-ite
Circa: 1930s
Value: $40-$60

Esso lighters.
Manufacturer: Zippo
Circa: 1940s
Value: $40-$50

Esso lighters.
Manufacturer: Zippo
Circa: 1950s
Value: $35-$60

Esso Happy Oil Drop lighters.
Manufacturers: Kaycee, Gas, Warco
Circa: 1960
Value: $40-$60

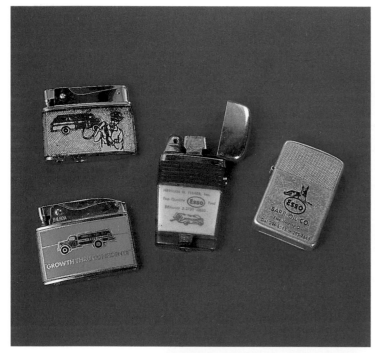

Esso lighters.
Manufacturers: Scripto and
others.
Circa: 1960s
Value: $25-$40

Esso lighters. One of these lighters has Essolite in the oval.
Circa: 1930s
Value: $40-$75

Winged Esso lighters.
Circa: 1940s
Value: $50-$75

Esso Happy Oil Drop lighter.
Circa: 1960s
Value: $75-$100

Esso matches.
Circa: 1938
Value: $25-$40

Esso lighters.
Manufacturer: Zippo
Circa: 1960s
Value: $35-$60

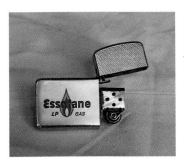

Essotane lighter.
Manufacturer: Zippo
Circa: 1960
Value: $25-$35

Esso matches.
Circa: 1930s-1950s
Value: $2-$5

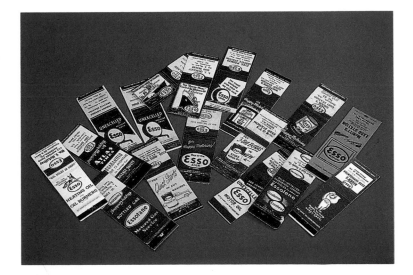

Esso Manhattan lighter. Everyone who took the
historic voyage to the Northwest Passage aboard the
tanker Manhattan received one of these lighters.
Manufacturer: Zippo
Circa: 1967
Value: $50-$100

Esso matches.
Circa: 1930s-1950s
Value: $2-$5

Esso matches. These items are related to the Army-Navy football game. The matches show a position on each match
Circa: 1936
Value: $25-$35

Esso ashtray. The back of this ashtray reads "First Commercial Iron Made With Oil Dofasco November 1960."
Material: Iron
Circa: 1960
Value: No Estimate

Esso matches. These matches were given to each attendee at the grand opening of the Esso Region office on York Road in Towson, Maryland.
Circa: 1949
Value: $25-$30

Esso ashtray with drum bung seal.
Material: Glass
Circa: 1950s
Value: $25-$50

Esso ashtray.
Material: Glass
Circa: 1966
Value: $25-$50

Esso ashtray.
Material: Metal
Circa: 1940s
Value: $20-$40

Wax

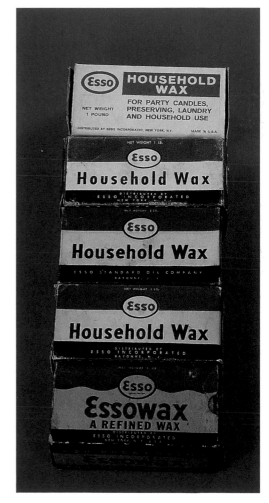

Esso wax.
Size: 1-pound
Circa: 1930s-1960s
Value: $8-$10

Essotane ashtray.
Material: Metal
Circa: 1960s
Value: $20-$30

Esso wax.
Size: .25-pound
Circa: 1930s-1950s
Value: $5-$10

Coin Banks

Esso coin banks. The two banks on the left are Humble. The far left bank is the narrow band oval and the bank in the middle is the wide band oval. The Esso bank on the right is a narrow band variety.
Material: Plastic
Circa: Left 1950s; Middle 1965; Right 1950s
Value: $75-$100; $75-$100; $75-$100

Esso bank. "Buy At The Esso Sign."
Material: Plastic
Circa: 1950s
Value: $75-$100

Esso New York Worlds Fair bank.
Material: Glass
Circa: 1939
Value: $65-$85

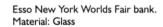

Esso banks. Because of the success of the World's Fair Bank, when World War II broke out Esso decided to make a bank to encourage people to save their money to buy war bonds to help finance the war effort.
Material: Glass
Circa: 1943
Value: $60-$100

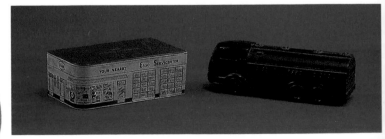

Esso banks. The one on the left is a service station bank and the one on the right is a tank truck bank.
Material: Plastic
Circa: 1950s
Value: $30-$50

Esso Happy Oil Drop bank, blue. This is the only example of a blue Happy Oil Drop bank to surface. It is felt that perhaps this was a sample that was not accepted for manufacture, possibly a specimen or a trial color. Chances are, no one will ever know for sure. It would answer a lot of questions if more would surface.
Material: Plastic
Circa: 1960s
Value: No Estimate

Esso Happy Oil Drop bank, red.
Material: Plastic
Circa: 1960s
Value: $75-$110

Esso Happy Oil Drop bank, white.
Material: Plastic
Circa: 1960s
Value: $120-$150

Esso Gas Pump Glass Advertising Panels

The following pump panels fit different gas pumps, although no attempt is made here to identify which pump they fit. These panels all fit electric pumps of different manufacturers. The value estimate is for one panel even though it is understood that each pump takes two.

Esso bank.
Material: Plastic
Circa: 1950s
Value: $20-$30

Esso Extra Marine.
Size: 12.5" x 5"
Circa: 1950s
Value: $15-$20

New Esso Extra and Esso Extra. The New Esso Extra panel was the first Esso Extra panel to be used in a pump. Esso Extra gasoline was introduced in 1939 and all advertising referred to the product as New.
Size: New Esso Extra 12.5" x 5"; Esso Extra 10.25" x 4.25"
Value: $35-$50; $25-$35
Circa: 1939; 1940s

Esso Extra. The bottom panel was only used in Texas.
Size: Top 12.5" x 5"; Bottom 10.75" x 4.75"
Value: $15-$20; $15-$20
Circa: 1940s; 1950s

Esso Tractor Fuel and Esso Diesel.
Size: Both 12.5" x 5"
Circa: 1940s
Value: $20-$30

Essofleet. As the name implies Essofleet Premium is the premium fuel and Essofleet is the regular fuel.
Size: 12.5" x 5"
Circa: 1940s-1950s
Value: $20-$30

Esso Marine. The blue panel is premium gasoline. The red panel is regular gasoline.
Size: 12.5" x 5"
Circa: 1950s
Value: $20-$30

Esso Extra.
Size: 12.5" x 5"
Circa: Top 1950s; Bottom 1940s
Value: $20-$30 each

Esso Extra and Golden Esso Extra. Golden was a super premium gasoline introduced in 1956 and was sold until about 1963. This was the beginning of the three grade gasoline system we see in just about every gasoline station today.
Size: 12.5" x 5"
Circa: 1950s-1960s
Value: Top $15-$20; Bottom $25-$30

Esso Plus and Esso Extra. Esso Plus replaced Golden but it was not a super premium gasoline. Rather, it became the mid-grade between Esso and Esso Extra. It was a simple task to convert every station since the third underground tank was already installed.
Size: 12.5" x 5"
Circa: 1960s-1970s
Value: $15-$20

Esso.
Size: 12.5" x 5"
Circa: 1930s-1970s
Value: $15-$20

Esso Kerosene.
Size: 12.5" x 5"
Circa: Top 1940s; Bottom 1950s
Value: $30-$40; $20-$30

Pin Back Buttons

Employee badge from Bayway, New Jersey refinery.
Circa: 1940s
Value: $50-$100

Employee badges from Bayonne, New Jersey refinery and Baytown, Texas refinery.
Circa: 1930s-1940s
Value: $75-$125

Kesbec Service Station attendant's badge. Standard Oil Company's affiliate, Colonial Beacon Oil Company, acquired 75 percent of Kesbec, Inc. stock in 1931. Kesbec was a company that owned and operated fifty-five service stations in Westchester County, New York, in the boroughs of Manhattan and the Bronx in New York City, and on Long Island.
Circa: 1930s
Value: $150-$200

Baltimore refinery employee badge.
Circa: 1940s
Value: $50-$100

It Pays To Use Esso pin back.
Circa: 1920s
Value: $75-$100

Aerotype Esso pin back.
Circa: 1931
Value: $75-$100

Happy Motoring pin backs.
Circa: 1940s
Value: $35-$50

Ask For Esso Extra pin back.
Circa: 1940s
Value: $50-$75

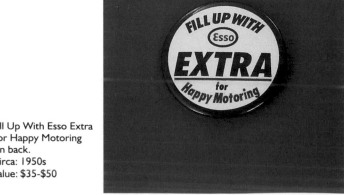

Fill Up With Esso Extra For Happy Motoring pin back.
Circa: 1950s
Value: $35-$50

Esso Happy Motoring Service pin back.
Circa: 1950s
Value: $35-$50

Use Essolube Today pin back.
Circa: 1930s
Value: $50-$75

Esso is Doing More pin back.
Circa: 1960s
Value: $30-$40

Esso and Esso Extra pin backs.
Circa: 1940
Value: $35-$50

Esso Cumberland (Maryland) Car Race Infield pin backs.
Circa: 1960s
Value: $25-$30 Each

Buy At The Esso sign with
Santa Claus and Merry
Christmas.
Circa: 1930s
Value: $50-$60

Esso Happy Motoring Merry
Christmas pin back.
Circa: 1940s
Value: $50-$60

Dr. Seuss character, "Meet
Gus." On the back side of this
celluloid button is Happy
Motoring! "Standard" Esso
Dealer.
Circa: 1930s
Value: $200-$350

Penn-Esso Employees Associa-
tion 1973.
Circa: 1973
Value: $25-$50

Credit Cards and Charge Plates

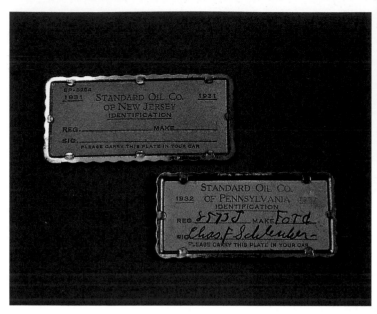

Standard Oil Company of New Jersey and Standard Oil Company of Pennsylvania Charge-A-Plates.
Circa: 1931-1932
Value: $150-$200

It is unknown just when the first credit cards were issued by Standard Oil Company of New Jersey. The earliest card I have is dated 1932, which is probably the beginning since I also have a Charge-A-Plate dated 1931. I know there is a Charge-A-Plate dated 1930 used by Colonial Beacon Oil Company, which was a subsidiary of SONJ. Humble Oil and Refining Company issued credit cards starting in the 1920s. I have a Humble card that is undated but has a picture of a Visible Pump with a Globe that says Flashlike on it. I have to believe that this card was issued in the 1920s. I also know that the first Humble cards had Dixie Oil Company on them and were used by Humble employees in 1923. However, I don't think SONJ would have had both credit cards and Charge-A-Plates at the same time other than one transition year.

Paper charge cards. Originally, charge cards were issued in paper form and the transaction had to be recorded by hand.
Circa: 1932-1949
Value: $50-$75

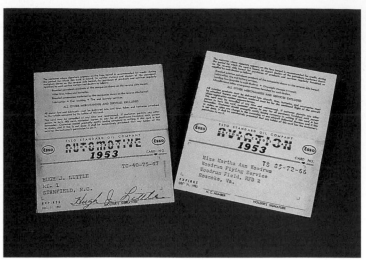

Paper credit cards. In 1953, Esso issued both automotive as well as aviation credit cards. Today one card can be used for the purchase of either fuel.
Circa: 1953
Value: $50-$75

Esso paper cards And holders. Beginning about 1938, Esso put their cards in a plastic holder with a calendar for that year. They stopped the calendars about 1942 but continued sending a plastic holder every time they issued customers a new card.
Circa: 1948-1950
Value: $50-$75

Esso paper card holders. Here are some more examples of the paper card holders.
Material: Plastic
Circa: 1938-1953
Value: $10-$15

Essomatic credit card machine. This was the second machine the company used, which was an improvement over the 1954 machine (shown below left). It was easier to service because the top lifted up completely to allow for changing the worn dealer ID plate and you could also change the ink rolls more easily. The handle was located on top and rolled much more smoothly than the "plunger type" from 1954.
Circa: 1958
Value: $150-$175

Esso paper card mailer. This is a beautiful example of a mailer that was used to send a customer his new credit card at Christmas. The inscription inside reads "May the enclosed credit card serve to bring you many miles of Happy Motoring throughout Nineteen Forty-Two" Esso Marketers.
Size: 8.5" x 3.75"
Circa: 1942
Value: $50-$60

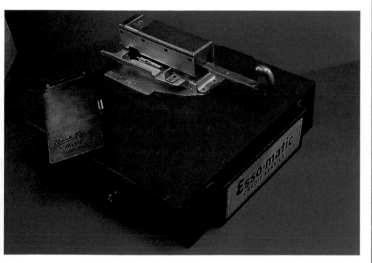

Essomatic credit card machine. In 1954, Esso issued a new type credit card. This one was a combination of paper and metal. The paper card was enclosed in a clear plastic "pouch" and a metal plate was attached to the heavy plastic pouch. When the customer made a purchase the attendant simply put the card in this machine and pulled a handle, causing an ink roller (there was no carbon paper then) to roll across the metal plate which had the customer's name and address and record the sale. This was much more accurate then the previous system of hand recording every sale. The Esso salesman carried a supply of ink rollers and kept the station supplied.
Circa: 1954
Value: $150-$175, complete with base

1954 pouch credit card. This is the first card designed to be used in the new credit card machines. Notice the direction arrows which showed how the card was to be inserted in the machine.
Circa: 1954
Value: $35-$50

Plastic credit card. In 1958, another change took place. Now that the company had the credit card machine, all they had to do was change the card to make things better. Instead of a heavy plastic "pouch," Esso did away with the metal plate and embossed the plastic holder itself with the customer's account number, name, and address.
Circa: 1958
Value: $35-$50

Plastic credit cards. In 1961, the company went to all plastic with no paper card at all.
Circa: 1961
Value: $25-$30

Plastic credit cards. Cards were issued for Esso, Humble, and Enco since these were the three operating brands.
Value: $20-$25

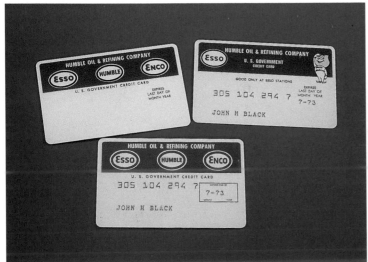

Plastic credit cards.
Circa: 1963-1970
Value: $20-$25

Plastic credit cards. These cards were issued to customers outside the Esso marketing territory.
Circa: 1962-1966
Value: $20-$25

Plastic credit cards. These are more examples of different cards that were issued through the years.
Circa: 1965-1970
Value: $10-$20

Plastic credit cards. These cards were replaced with the new Exxon cards that came out in 1972. However, some of the Humble cards had been issued with expiration dates that went as far as 1974 and these were honored at all Exxon stations.
Circa: 1965-1974
Value: $10-$20

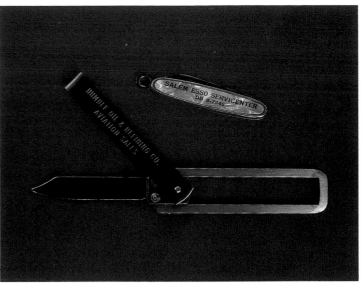

Knives

Esso knives. Some of Esso's distributors and service station dealers produced their own knives with their own name and address for distribution to their own customers.
Circa: 1960s
Value: Top $15-$25; Bottom $25-$35

Esso knife. The handles of this knife actually fold over the blade.
Circa: 1950s
Value: $25-$30

For the most part, knives with the Esso logo were manufactured to be given away to the company's customers as thank you gifts for using their products.

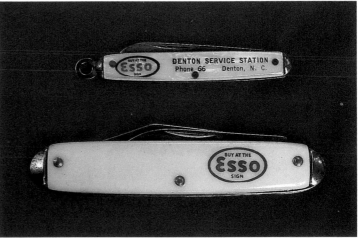

Esso knives. The knife shown at the top is an example of a service station dealer producing his own knife for distribution to his customers.
Circa: 1930s
Value: Top $35-$50; Bottom $50-$75

Esso knives. The knife at the top has a blade that goes straight out and retracts directly into the handle. The knife below is also a letter opener.
Circa: 1950s
Value: Top $15-$20; Bottom $35-$50

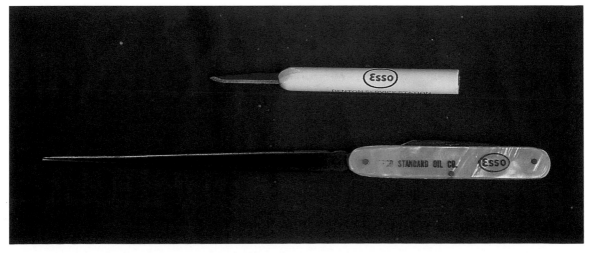

Esso Happy Oil Drop knife.
Circa: 1960
Value: $75-$100

Esso G&B 96 gas pump knife.
Circa: 1940s
Value: $75-$100

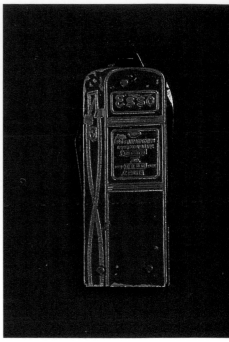

Esso G&B 996 gas pump knife.
Circa: 1950s
Value: $50-$75

Esso gas pump knife. Here are three
different styles of the same knife. Two
have the Essolube logo on the handle.
Circa: 1920s-1930s
Value: $75-$150 each

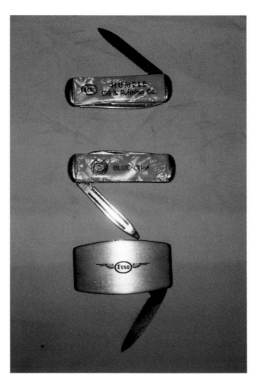

Esso knives.
Circa: 1950s
Value: $20-$30

Esso knife. This is a
two blade knife. One
blade is a finger nail file.
Circa: 1950s
Value: $35-$50

Toys

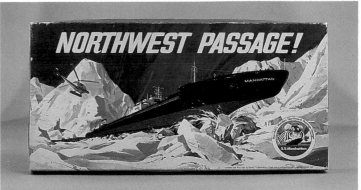

Northwest Passage board game.
Circa: 1970s
Value: $15-$25

Esso service station.
Material: Plastic
Circa: 1960
Value: $50-$70

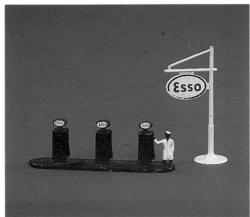

Esso pump island and sign.
Manufacturer: Lesney
Circa: 1960s
Value: $30-$50

This is a two-story Esso garage/service station with
Esso gas pump island from A-1 accessory pack.
Material: Plastic with metal pump island
Manufactorer: Matchbox MG-1B-1
Circa: 1950s
Value: $100-$200

Esso double-decker buses. There
are three colors: red, white, and
green.
Manufacturer: Lesney
Circa: 1960s
Value: $10-$20

Esso tank trucks.
Manufacturer: Lesney
Circa: 1960s
Value: $30-$60

Essolube tank wagon.
Manufacturer: Dinky Toys
Circa: 1930s
Value: $100-$150

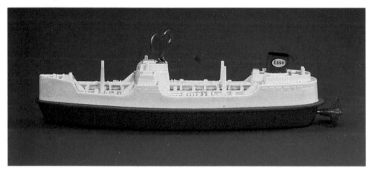

Esso double-decker buses.
Manufacturer: Budgie
Circa: 1960
Value: $15-$25

Esso aviation fuel truck.
Manufacturer: Bungie
Circa: 1950s
Value: $75-$100

Esso ship.
Manufacturer: Lehmann
Circa: 1950s
Value: $25-$40

Esso tank wagon.
Manufacturer: Tekno
Circa: 1930s
Value: $50-$75

Esso toy truck banks, red and clear.
Circa: 1950s
Value: Red $25-35; Clear $50-$60

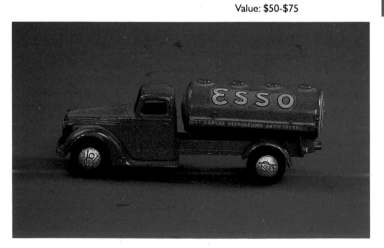

More Miscellaneous

Esso lapel pin. This lapel pin was worn by a member of the marine department. It shows an Esso logo on a flag, which was a typical symbol for the marine department.
Size: 1" wide x 1.5" long
Circa: 1940s
Value: $15-$25

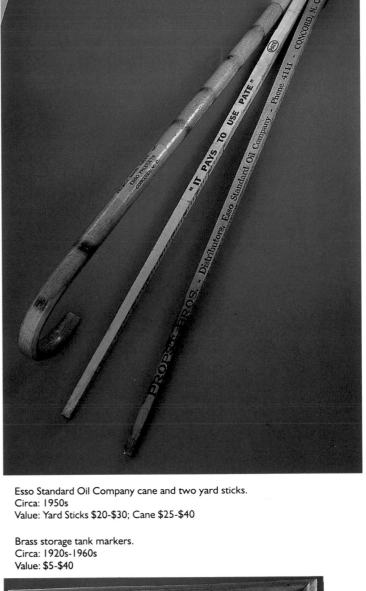

Esso Standard Oil Company cane and two yard sticks.
Circa: 1950s
Value: Yard Sticks $20-$30; Cane $25-$40

Brass storage tank markers.
Circa: 1920s-1960s
Value: $5-$40

Esso Babe Ruth Boys Club membership badge. Esso paid Babe Ruth, a famous baseball player of the 1910s and 1920s, for the use of his name to promote the game of baseball and to begin at an early time getting Esso's name in front of future customers.
Size: 1.25"
Circa: 1920s
Value: $20-$50

Esso female Happy Oil Drop candle. The female version of Happy Oil Drop was never given an official name.
Size: 5"
Circa: 1960s
Value: $5-$25

Esso license plate attachment.
Circa: 1950s
Value: $10-$40

Esso windshield service box. These boxes were placed on the service islands and contained materials which were used by the attendant to clean your windshield.
Circa: 1950s
Value: $100-$150

Above: Esso license plate attachment.
Circa: 1930s
Value: $30-$60

Below: Esso Santa Claus mailbox. These mailboxes were placed in service stations for the use of customers' children. The child would write a letter to Santa Claus and place it in the mailbox. Each child would receive a reply.
Circa: 1950s
Value: $100-$150

Esso windshield service bottle. This spray bottle was filled with cleaner and was also equipped with a bug brush, which was used by the attendant to clean your windshield.
Circa: 1950s
Value: $10-$25

Mistol. This was a product used as a nose drop to relieve nasal congestion.
Circa: 1930s
Value: $5-$25

Esso gas pump lighter fluid dispenser. These pumps were usually found on counters in the lobbies of Esso office buildings for the convenience of visitors calling on personnel in the buildings.
Size: 3.5" x 10"
Circa: 1950s
Value: $250-$500

Esso cups.
Circa: 1960s
Value: $1-$5

Esso cup and furnace ID oval.
Circa: 1960s
Value: $1-$25

Esso World War II cigarette box.
Size: 1.75" x 3.75"
Circa: 1940s
Value: No Estimate

This simple cigarette box is an example of defiance and resistance shown by employees of the company's Norwegian affiliate to Nazi occupation forces during World War II. It bears evidence of an obvious yet clever ruse that outsmarted German forces in Norway during the war.

During the occupation period, it was reported, tobacco was stringently rationed and the company therefore obtained permission to have tobacco grown and manufactured for employees. Packaged with the company name, English was used on the front and back with Norwegian (or so the Germans thought) on the sides. The cigarettes, needless to say, found their way far beyond the employees.

What the Germans never seemed to realize was that though the lettering on the sides of the package was indeed Norwegian and said simply "home-rolled"—a common enough term—the message it actually carried was in English and meant "home rule," the watchword for courage and resistance to Nazi dictatorship.

Esso attendants' caps.
Circa: Left 1950s; Right 1960s
Value: $25-$50; $20-$40

Esso warehouseman's apron.
Circa: 1950s
Value: $30-$50

Golden Esso Extra bumper sticker. This was a super premium gasoline that was introduced in 1956.
Circa: 1950s
Value: $10-$20

Above: Esso Happy Oil Drop hand puppet.
Material: Rubber
Circa: 1960s
Value: $15-$25

Below: Esso Happy Motoring utility bag.
Circa: 1950s
Value: $30-$60

Nosey figurine. This was given as an award for selling odorless mineral spirits solvent.
Size: 5.5" tall
Circa: 1960s
Value: $50-$100

Esso Happy Oil Drop figurine. This was given as an award by the oil heat department for new sales.
Size: 8" tall
Circa: 1960s
Value: $50-$150

Esso mirrors. These mirrors were given to service station customers. They attached to the sun visor of your car much like the ones that are built in to our cars today.
Circa: 1940s-1950s
Value: $25-$50

Esso sales receipt box.
Circa: 1950s
Value: $30-$50

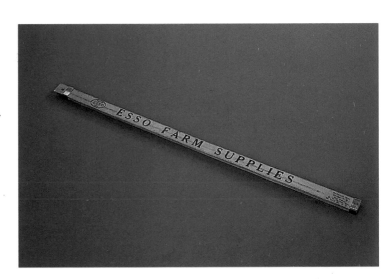

Esso Farm Supplies yard stick.
Circa: 1930s
Value: $30-$50

Esso marine jacket buttons.
Circa: 1950s
Value: $40-$50

Esso neckties. These were given as gifts to favorite customers and also to employees.
Circa: 1960s
Value: $15-$30

Esso Extra printers block. These blocks were used by printers to produce stationery. There are many other styles of Esso printer's blocks that were used during this period as well.
Circa: 1960s
Value: $15-$20

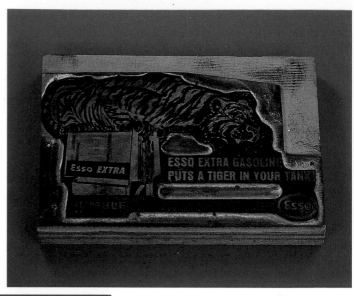

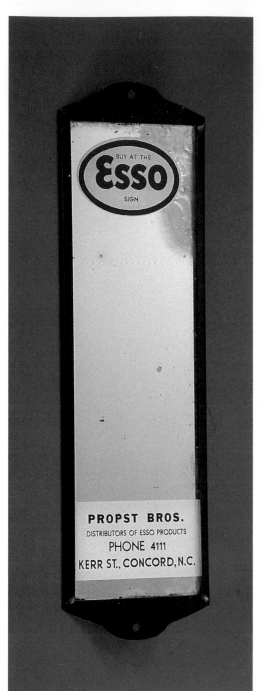

Esso mirror door push.
Circa: 1930s
Value: $35-$50

Esso rest room key tag holder.
Material: Plastic
Circa: 1960s
Value: $50-$75

Esso men's key tag.
Material: Plastic
Circa: 1960s
Value: $35-$50

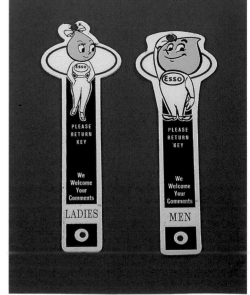

Esso Happy Oil Drop and female Happy key tags.
Material: Plastic
Circa: 1960s
Value: $75-$100

Dr. Seuss Navy "Grog" glasses. Each year, the Seuss Navy held "Annual Maneuvers." These maneuvers took place at a different location each year. Each "Admiral" (every member was an Admiral) received a set of Grog glasses to take home as a souvenir of the meeting.
Size: 12 ounce
Circa: 1939-1940
Value: $10-$30

Esso belt buckles.
Circa: 1930s-1940s
Value: Brass $50-$60; Cloisonné $50-$75

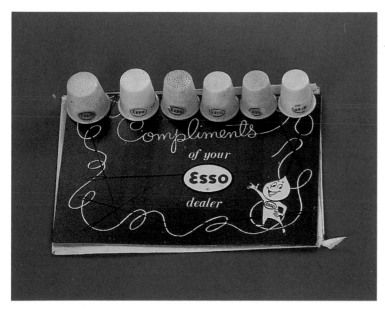

Esso needle pack and thimbles.
Circa: 1960s
Value: Needle Pack $10-$20; Thimbles $5-$10

Esso clock. Most clocks were produced by distributors of Esso products and not Esso. This is an example.
Circa: 1950s
Value: $50-$75

Essolene belt buckle.
Manufacturer: Hamlin Belt Co., Greensboro, North Carolina
Circa: 1930s
Value: $50-$100

Esso salt and pepper shakers with box
Circa: 1950s
Value: $40-$50

Esso oil can rack.
Circa: 1940s
Value: $50-$100

Esso oil burner. Esso sold and serviced oil burners as a part of their Home Heating Oil Service.
Circa: 1950s
Value: $30-$60

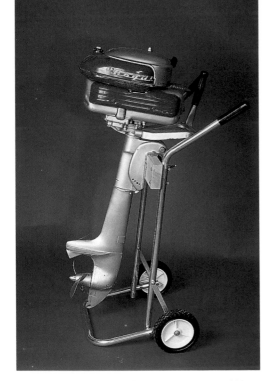

Royal outboard motor. These motors were sold by Atlas Supply Company and were available at Esso Stations in various horsepowers.
Circa: 1940s
Value: $125-$200

Esso watchdog. This was the symbol of Esso's Watchdog Oil Heat Service. These dogs were mounted on the cabs of service trucks and were very impressive when the trucks would make their way down the street.
Size: 43" x 13" x 21"
Material: Rubber
Circa: 1950s
Value: $600-$1200

Put a Tiger in Your Tank! The Esso Tiger is Introduced in the United States.

Esso Tiger bank.
Circa: 1960s
Value: $30-$50

In the spring of 1964, the most successful roll out of an oil company ad campaign occurred. It was then that the Esso Tiger was introduced to the U S. To say that the campaign was an instant success would be an understatement, yet it did not happen by chance; every move was skillfully calculated. The campaign was initiated in the spring, for example, because spring was perceived to be the prime driving season. Teaser ads were the first order of business. They proclaimed that "A Tiger Is Coming To Town" and the illustration showed nothing more than the Tiger's head peering around the edge of the paper. The ad bore no other identification except an Esso oval which was only a logo mark. The second teaser was a little more specific, for it identified the Tiger with a product. While the headline remained the same as in the first, the illustration now portrayed a whiskery face emerging from the top of an Esso Extra pump. But the Tiger was impatient to be loose; the next ads in the press revealed him in his full glory as conceived by Bob Jones, the artist collaborating with McCann's (advertising company in charge of the roll out). There he stood, elbow resting on an Esso Extra pump, whiskers ruffled by the draft of an unseen car he had clearly just sent roaring on its way. "Now. Great New Esso Extra!" screamed the headline, and below the beast himself, "Put a Tiger in Your Tank!" In a piece of hardworking copy the full promise of the Tiger's powers was dramatically proclaimed. At the foot of the ad, beside the Esso oval, the baseline read in small type: "Humble Oil & Refining Company, America's leading energy company, makers of Esso products."

The merchandising activity likewise came into full swing. Humble service stations began to offer a variety of promotional items both for sale and as giveaways: coloring books (which also included a story about the Tiger), fluffy Tigers dolls, key rings, party glasses, etc. The notable exception to the list is, of course, the item which ended up being the most prominent of all: the Tiger Tail. Curiously, it had not been figured in the original merchandising plan; in fact, it had not even been thought of. Soon after the campaign began, Humble was approached by an independent textile manufacturer who asked if they would agree to their offering Tiger Tails to some of the service stations for use as a further promotional gimmick. With Humble's consent, a small supply was arranged; this supply disappeared so rapidly that subcontractors had to be brought in almost immediately to help meet what was to become an overwhelming demand. Less than five months from the beginning of the Tiger's launch, Humble dealers had already given away five hundred thousand key chains and had sold 3.5 million Tiger Tails, 2.5 million Tiger coloring books and two hundred thousand Tiger dolls.

Over the years, countless Tiger items that were either sold or given away during these fantastically successful years from 1964-1969 have continued to surface. Some, but certainly not all, are shown on the following pages.

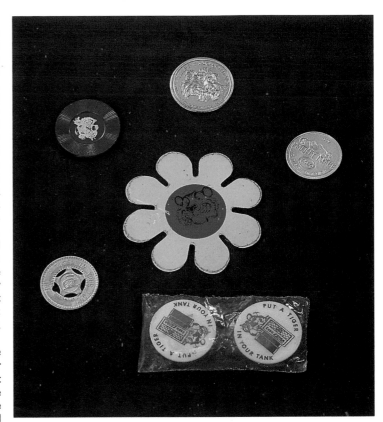

Tiger assortment.
Circa: 1960s
Value: $1-$10

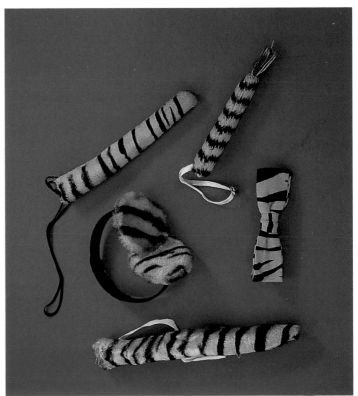

Tiger tails, ear muff, and bow tie.
Circa: 1960s
Value: Tiger tails $1-$5; Ear muff $5-$10; Bow tie $5-$10

Tiger key chains. The tiger heads on the perimeter were issued by the credit card center as a way of recovering lost car keys for credit card holders.
Circa: 1960
Value: $1-$5

Tiger fan.
Circa: 1960s
Value: $10-$15

Tiger assortment.
Circa: 1960s
Value: $1-$8

Tiger pillow.
Circa: 1960s
Value: $10-$15

Tiger assortment.
Circa: 1960s
Value: $1-$15

Tiger serving tray.
Circa: 1960s
Value: $10-$15

Above: Tiger glasses.
Circa: 1960s
Value: $10-$15

Below: Tiger pitcher and matching glass.
Circa: 1960s
Value: Pitcher $35-$50; Glass $10-$15

Two different tiger pitchers. These are the two other Tiger pitchers with accompanying glass. These two are known as the "Sausage Tiger" because of the long body.
Circa: 1960s
Value: $35-$50 per pitcher

Below: Two different tiger pitchers. I have identified four different Tiger pitchers; each has an accompanying glass.
Circa: 1960s
Value: $35-$50 per pitcher

Tiger assortment.
Circa: 1960s
Value: $10-$25

Tiger assortment.
Circa: 1960s
Value: $5-$30

Tiger key chains.
Circa: 1960s
Value: $10-$35

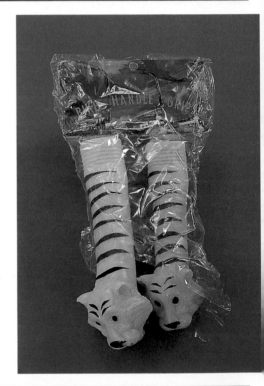

Tiger handlebar grips.
Circa: 1960s
Value: $25-$50

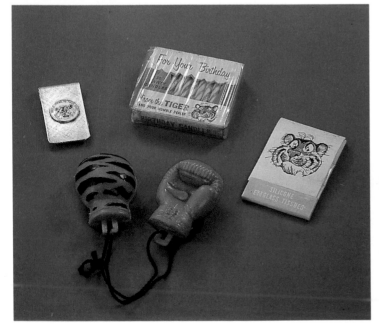

Tiger assortment.
Circa: 1960s
Value: $5-$30

Tiger assortment.
Circa: 1960s
Value: $5-$10

Tiger assortment.
Circa: 1960s
Value: $5-$20

Tiger jacket patch.
Circa: 1960s
Value: $15-$25

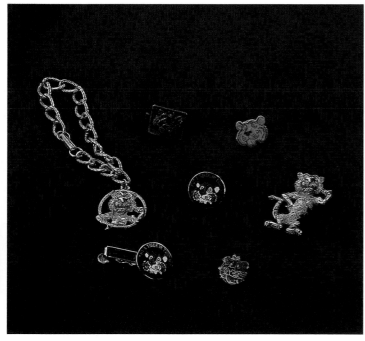

Tiger jewelry and necktie pins.
Circa: 1960s
Value: $5-$50

Tiger lighters.
Circa: 1960s
Value: $35-$50

Tiger coin bank.
Circa: 1960s
Value: $20-$35

Chapter 3

Humble Oil and Refining Company

In 1917, nine men with an average age of less than forty years, seven of whom had spent their entire working lives finding and producing oil, organized the Humble Oil and Refining Company. Confident about the future of the oil industry in Texas and ambitious to grow with it, they combined their resources in order to more effectively and profitably develop the business of producing oil. On January 29, 1919, Standard Oil Company (NJ) acquired fifty percent of the outstanding stock and Humble was on its way to expansion. Jersey was so impressed with the men of Humble that two of the original organizers went on to become President of Jersey Standard. In 1920-21 the company built a one million dollar building in the center of Houston, occupying half a city block and rising nine stories. The company's current building is still in Houston and was opened in 1962. At six hundred feet high and forty-four floors it is quite a contrast to the structure of 1920.

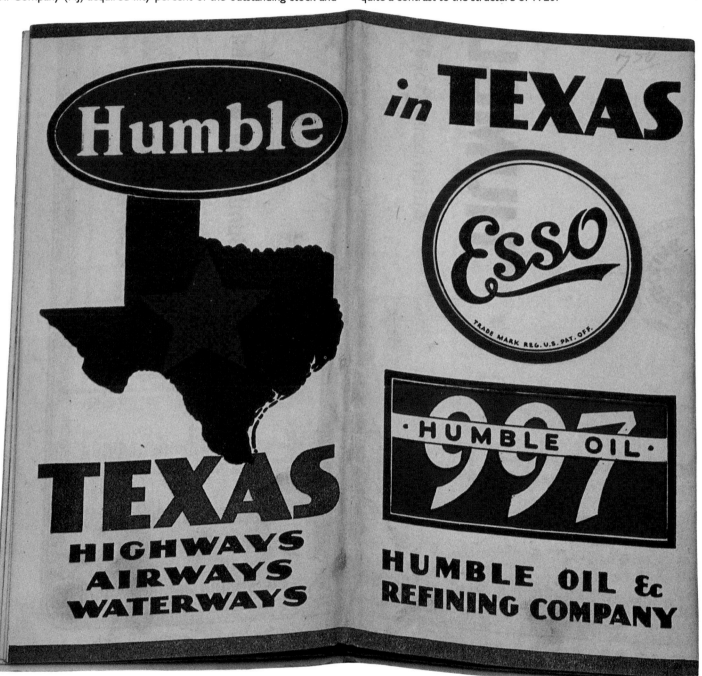

Map of Texas

Flashlike ethyl gas pump metal band globe. This was the premium grade gasoline sold by Humble in the 1920s until July of 1931 when Esso replaced it.
Size: 15"
Circa: 1920s-1931
Value: $450-$650

Humble oils (external gear) metal band gas pump globe. This globe was the regular grade gasoline used by Humble in the 1920s.
Size: 15"
Circa: 1920s
Value: $650-$900

Humble bar and circle gas pump metal band globe. This was the regular grade gasoline sold by Humble in the 1930s.
Size: 15"
Circa: 1930s
Value: $500-$800

Humble metal band gas pump globe. This globe was the regular grade gasoline used in the 1940s.
Size: 15"
Circa: 1940s
Value: $450-$550

Humble gasoline (internal gear) Humble oils plastic body globe. This was not a gas pump globe. It was designed to be used as a window display.
Size: 13.5"
Circa: 1950s
Value: $350-$500

Thriftane metal band gas pump globe. This was a sub-regular (low octane) gasoline introduced in January, 1939. The product was used as tractor fuel and for cars that did not require regular grade octane fuel.
Size: 15"
Circa: 1930s
Value: $350-$500

Signs

National A38 pump with Thriftane glass inserts.
Type: Electric
Circa: 1936
Value: $800-$1,000

Uniflo Motor Oil pump topper sign. This sign is two sided with adhesive on the bottom to attach to the gas pump. Note that the word Esso is covered up by the All Weather banner. That meant that it could be used in states that would not allow the brand Esso but had no problem with the name Uniflo.
Circa: 1960s
Value: $30-$60

Red background porcelain Humble pump sign.
Size: 18" x 11"
Circa: 1930s
Value: $75-$125

Esso Extra porcelain
pump sign.
Size: 18" x 11"
Circa: 1950s
Value: $75-$125

FIRST AID

THIS STATION IS PROVIDED WITH
A FIRST AID KIT THE CONTENTS OF
WHICH ARE AVAILABLE TO YOU IN
CASE OF ACCIDENT OR INJURY. THESE
FACILITIES ARE OFFERED AS A CON-
VENIENCE TO YOU AT NO CHARGE.

FIRE PROTECTION

THE FIRE EXTINGUISHERS AT THIS
SERVICE STATION ARE AVAILABLE FOR
YOUR USE IN CASE OF AUTOMOBILE
OR OTHER FIRE.

NOTE.
IN CASE OF NEED FOR FIRST AID OR ASSIS-
TANCE IN EXTINGUISHING A FIRE OUR SALES-
MEN WILL GLADLY COOPERATE TO THE BEST
OF THEIR ABILITY.

HUMBLE OIL & REFINING CO.

First aid and fire protection
porcelain sign.
Size: 9" x 7"
Circa: 1940s
Value: $150-$200

White background
porcelain Humble
pump sign.
Size: 18" x 11"
Circa: 1940s
Value: $75-$100

Humble Gasoline Motor Oils Authorized Dealer porcelain sign.
Size: 42"
Circa: 1930s
Value: $150-$250

Red background porcelain rest room sign.
Size: 9" x 7"
Circa: 1930s-1940s
Value: $175-$250

White background porcelain rest room sign.
Size: 9" x 7"
Circa: 1940s-1950s
Value: $150-$200

For Your Safety We Don't Smoke On Drive Way porcelain sign. This sign was mounted on the outside of service stations as a reminder to their customers.
Size: 14" x 10"
Circa: 1940s-1950s
Value: $100-$175

Velvet Motor Oil embossed metal sign.
Size: 27.75" x 19.75"
Circa: 1930s
Value: $200-$300

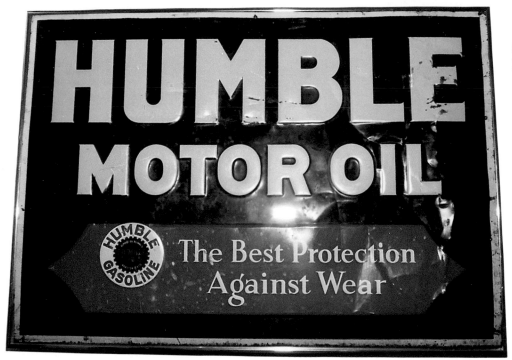

Humble Motor Oil embossed metal sign.
Size: 27.75" x 19.75"
Circa: 1930s
Value: $200-$300

997 Motor Oil porcelain sign.
Size: 111" x 35"
Circa: 1930s
Value: No Estimate

White background Humble porcelain sign.
Size: 52" x 26"
Circa: 1940s
Value: $100-$200

Humble Gasoline Humble Oils porcelain sign.
Size: 42"
Circa: 1940s-1950s
Value: $100-$200

Red background Humble porcelain sign.
Size: 12" x 6"
Circa: 1930s
Value: $150-$250

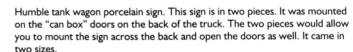

Humble tank wagon porcelain sign. This sign is in two pieces. It was mounted on the "can box" doors on the back of the truck. The two pieces would allow you to mount the sign across the back and open the doors as well. It came in two sizes.
Size: 36" x 18"; 47" x 23.5"
Value: $100-$200; $150-$250
Circa: 1940s-1950s

White background Humble porcelain truck sign. This sign was mounted on the doors of tank trucks.
Size: 14" x 7.25"
Circa: 1940s-1950s
Value: $150-$250

Red background Humble porcelain sign.
Size: 52" x 26"
Circa: 1930s
Value: $150-$250

White background Humble porcelain truck sign. This sign was mounted on the
doors of tank trucks.
Size: 10.5" x 7"
Circa: 1960s
Value: $150-$250

Authorized Dealer Agency Humble Oil & Refining Company. This is a wood framed painted metal sign that hung in front of
all distributor locations.
Size: 37" x 11"
Circa: 1930s-1940s
Value: $100-$200

Humble letters. These letters hung under the eves of Humble stations. In the old Esso marketing territory, the company
name had changed, and they were trying to get the Esso public to make an association with the name Humble. It was hoped
that just the name Humble would one day be used everywhere, but the name Exxon was chosen instead.
Size: 120" x 22"
Circa: 1960s-1970s
Value: $100-$150

Humble island light insert. This is an internally lit sign that fit in the canopies over the pump island.
Size: 18.5" x 14"
Circa: 1960s
Value: $100-$175

Esso More Powerful Than Any Gasoline. Even though it says Esso, this sign is included here because it was only used in Texas in the 1940s. Note that it is script Esso. This style Esso lettering was discontinued in the East Coast Esso territory in 1933.
Size: 36"
Circa: 1940s
Value: No Estimate

Humble porcelain sign.
Size: 36" x 18"
Circa: 1950s
Value: $150-$250

Happy Oil Drop porcelain sign.
Size: 46" x 25"
Circa: 1960s
Value: $500-$700

Cans

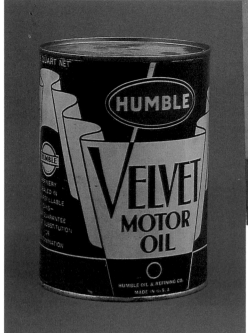

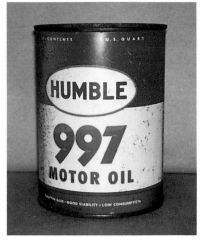

997 Motor Oil. In August, 1939 this product was reformulated and called "Improved, Balanced 997" with a new can design.
Circa: 1939
Size: 1-quart; 5-quart
Value: $30-$45; $45-$75

997 Motor Oil. This was the first can design change in the 1950s. Note that its white color carried over. Then, as noted below, the can was produced in a silver metallic cast design.
Size: 1-quart; 5-quart
Circa: 1950s
Value: $20-$30; $30-$40

Velvet Motor Oil. This product was introduced in September 1932 but was not available in round cans until 1934. In that year it was available in 1-quart and 5-quart sizes.
Size: 1-quart
Circa: 1930s
Value: $50-$75

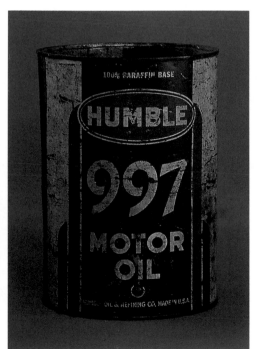

997 Motor Oil. After World War II, the product can design was changed to a white background Humble oval. The can in the center shows the first change. Note that the Humble oval still touches the first "9". Later, in the 1940s, the design was changed so the Humble oval cleared the "9" completely, as seen in the can on the left. In the 1950s, the can changed again for the last time, to a completely new design altogether. This can, shown on the right, has a silver metallic cast to it. Each can came in 1-quart and 5-quart size.
Position: Left; Center; Right
Size: 1-quart, 5-quart; 1-quart, 5-quart; 1-quart, 5-quart
Value: $25-$35, $35-$50; $25-$35, $35-$50; $20-$30, $30-40
Circa: 1940s-1950s

997 Motor Oil. This product made its first appearance in May, 1931 and was soon sweeping the state of Texas. It too was not available in round cans until 1934. This product was available in both 1-quart and 5-quart cans.
Circa: 1930s
Size: 1-quart; 5-quart
Value: $35-$50; $50-$100

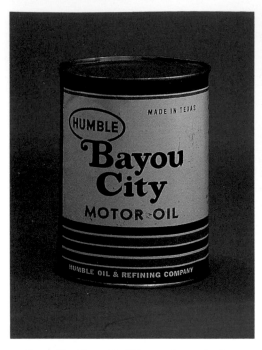

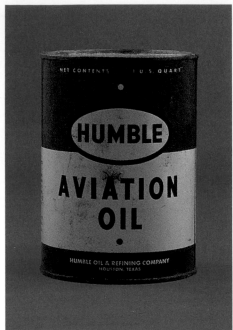

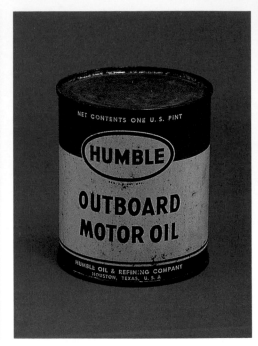

Bayou City Motor Oil. This was a low quality bulk type motor oil used in cars that were old and had high make up rates in the 1930s.
Size: 1-quart
Circa: 1930s
Value: $25-$35

Humble Aviation Oil.
Size: 1-quart
Circa: 1950s
Value: $10-$20

Humble Outboard Motor Oil.
Size: 1-pint
Circa: 1940s-1950s
Value: $10-$20

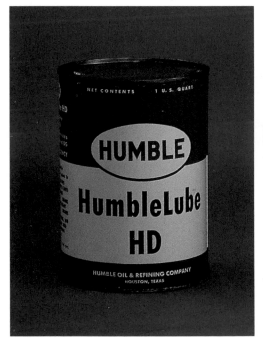

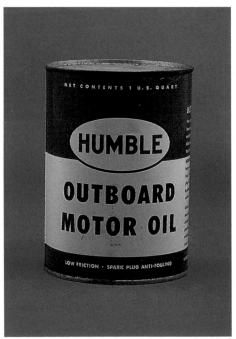

HumbleLube HD Motor Oil.
Size: 1-quart
Circa: 1950s
Value: $20-$30

Humble Outboard Motor Oil.
Size: 1-quart
Circa: 1950s
Value: $40-$50

Humble Aviation Oil.
Size: 1-gallon
Circa: 1950s
Value: $25-$50

Rust-Ban Thinner 360.
Size: 1-gallon
Circa: 1940s
Value: $15-$25

Humble enamel paint.
Size: 1-gallon
Circa: 1950s
Value: $20-$30

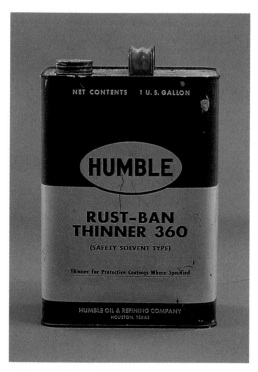

Rust-Ban Thinner 360.
Size: 1-gallon
Circa: 1950s
Value: $15-$25

Humble Varsol. This product was introduced in 1932 and soon became a household word. It was used by everyone to thin paint and for dry cleaning clothes.
Size: 2-gallon
Circa: 1932
Value: $50-$100

997 Motor Oil.
Size: 1-gallon
Circa: 1931
Value: No Estimate

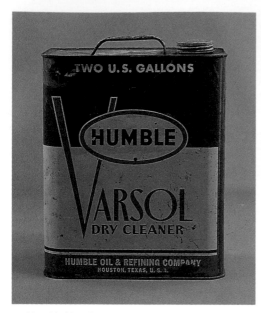

Humble Upper
Cylinder Oil.
Circa: 1950s
Size: 1-pint; 1-quart
Value: $10-$20;
$25-$35

Humble Varsol
Size: 2-gallon
Circa: 1940s-1950s
Value: $40-$75

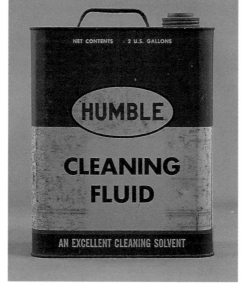

Humble Bayou City Motor Oil.
Size: 2-gallon
Circa: 1930s
Value: $50-$100

Humble Cleaning Fluid.
Size: 2-gallon
Circa: 1950s
Value: $25-$40

997 Motor Oil.
Size: 5-gallon
Circa: 1933
Value: $50-$100

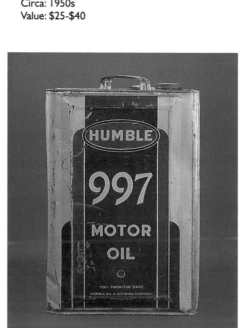

997 Motor Oil.
Size: 5-gallon
Circa: 1931
Value: $50-$100

Humble Appliance Gasoline.
Size: 5-gallon
Circa: 1940s
Value: $30-$60

Humble Household Lubricant. This can was
introduced in 1935.
Size: 4-ounce
Circa: 1935
Value: $50-$60

Humble Household Lubricant. This can also exists
with blue lettering at the bottom spelling out Handy
Oil.
Size: 4-ounce
Circa: 1940s
Value: $40-$60

Humble Products.
Size: 5-gallon
Circa: 1960s
Value: $25-$35

Humble Household Lubricant bottle. This
was a World War II bottle employed in order
to conserve metal for strategic war materials.
Size: 4-ounce
Circa: 1943-1945
Value: $125-$145

Humble Handy Oil.
Size: 4-ounce
Circa: 1960s
Value: $15-$20

Humble Household Lubricant. These cans are slightly different. The one on the right does not have REG. U.S. PAT. OFF. under the oval. There are also other differences as you can see.
Size: 4-ounce
Circa: 1940s-1950s
Value: $35-$50 each

Humble Handy Oil.
Size: 4-ounce
Circa: 1960s
Value: $15-$25

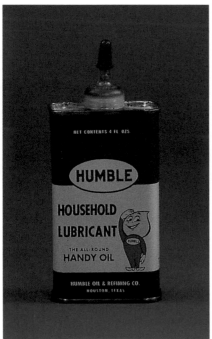

Humble Household Lubricant. This can was the beginning of the plastic spout cans.
Size: 4-ounce
Circa: 1950s
Value: $15-$25

Humble Household Lubricant. This can has the Happy Oil Drop on it. This is the only can I have seen in which Happy has on a blue outfit instead of white.
Size: 4-ounce
Circa: 1959-1960s
Value: $25-$35

Humble Flashlike lighter fluid. This product was first introduced in May, 1933.
Size: 4-ounce
Circa: 1950s
Value: $75-$100

Humble shadow letters Axle Grease Dark and Cup Grease Hard.
Size: 5-pounds; 10-pounds
Circa: 1930s
Value: $50-$75 each

Humble Rust-Ban 392.
Size: 4-ounce
Circa: 1940s-1950s
Value: $40-$60

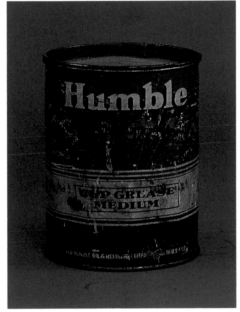

Humble shadow letters Cup Grease Medium.
Size: 1-pound
Circa: 1930s
Value: $25-$50

Humble shadow letters Cup Grease Medium. This can design was introduced early in the 1930s.
Size: 25-pounds
Circa: 1930s
Value: $50-$75

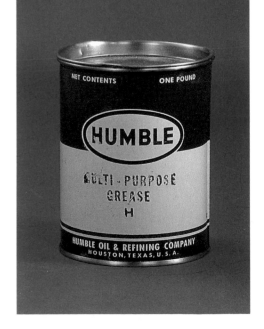

Humble Multi-Purpose Grease H.
Size: 1-pound
Circa: 1940s-1950s
Value: $25-$35

First Aid Kits

Humble first aid kit. First aid kits were found in all areas of the Humble Company much as you would find today. The kit featured here was probably found in a salesman's car since it is relatively small.
Size: 4" x 2"
Circa: 1930s
Value: $30-$40

Humble first aid kit.
Size: 8" x 4"
Circa: 1960s
Value: $50-$60

Humble first aid kit.
Size: 9.5" x 9.5"
Circa: 1940s
Value: $75-$100

Humble Esso Bearing Grease, Chassis Grease H, and Esso Chassis Grease H. Texas was a state that could fly the Esso banner unlike some other states where it was not permitted. Humble tried to leverage the success of the Esso brand by putting the name on some of their containers.
Size: (top)1-pound; (middle) 5-pound; (bottom)10-pound
Value: 1-pound $15-$25; 5-pound $20-$30; 10-pound $25-$35
Circa: 1940s-1950s

Humble first aid kit.
Size: 8" x 4"
Circa: 1950s
Value: $50-$75

Humble Esso Cup Grease.
Size: 1-pound
Circa: 1940s-1950s
Value: $15-$25

Smalls

Humble jacket patch, Eastern Region Distribution and Engineering.
Circa: 1972
Value: $25-$35

Humble Oil & Refining Company. This is a license plate attachment. It reads H. O. & R. Co. An employee who worked at a refinery or some other facility that required employees to identify themselves when they entered the gate probably used this type of attachment.
Size: 4.5" x 2.5"
Circa: 1930s
Value: No Estimate

Humble patches, various types.
Circa: 1930s-1960s
Value: $10 $20

Humble salt and pepper shakers. Gas pump design with box.
Circa: 1950s
Value: $65-$100

Humble wet stone or knife sharpening stone. This was an advertising giveaway to customers. This design also exists with a mirror instead of a sharpening stone. One appealed to men and the other to women.
Size: 2.75" x 1.75"
Circa: 1930s
Value: $50-$75

Humble no.1 toy oil rigs. This toy came out in the early 1960s and was a big hit with children and the motoring public alike.
Size: 3.5" x 8.25" x 8"
Circa: 1961
Value: $20-$30

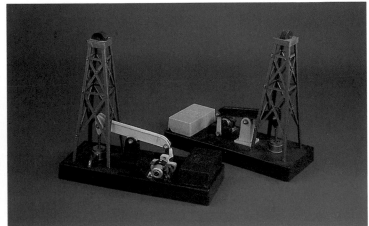

Happy rest room key holders.
Material: Metal
Circa: 1960
Value: $50-$100

Humble paper clip.
This was a customer
giveaway.
Circa: 1950s
Value: $5-$10

Humble pocket knife.
Circa: 1930s
Value: $75-$125

Humble matches. These matches were given away to announce the introduction of the worlds first multi-viscosity motor oil in 1952, Uniflo.
Size: 1.5" x 2.25"
Circa: 1952
Value: $45-$65

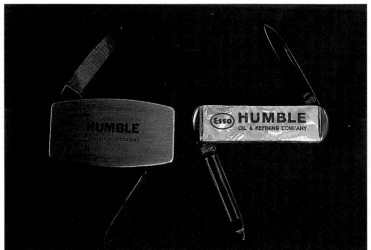

Humble pocket knives.
Circa: Left 1970; Right 1960s
Value: $20-$30 each

Humble paper credit card. This card is not dated but it has a picture of a visible gas pump with a Flashlike pump globe on top. I believe it is a 1929 or earlier card.
Circa: 1929
Value: $75-$100

Humble used paper credit cards until 1954 when a combination paper and metal card was issued (pouch card) to be used in the new Humblematic credit card machines. Then, in 1958, a combination paper and plastic card was issued. It could be used in the Humblematic machines as well. In 1960, a new all plastic card was produced and plastic cards have been used ever since.

Humble Fire Chief hat. Every fuel distribution terminal places emphasis on fire safety and fire drills are held on a regular basis. Each terminal has a Fire Chief who has responsibility for coordinating this activity in addition to his regular duties. This is a hat worn by one of the Fire Chiefs.
Circa: 1960s
Value: $75-$100

Humble rest room mirror. These mirrors were found in every rest room at Humble service stations throughout Texas.
Size: 22" x 14"
Circa: 1940s-1960s
Value: $150-$200

Humble paper credit cards, various years.
Circa: 1950s
Value: $35-$50

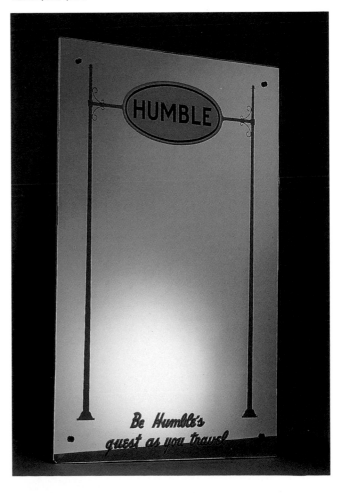

Humble credit card application box.
Material: Metal
Size: 8" x 6"
Circa: 1960s
Value: $50-$100

Humble rest room check card. These boxes were in the rest rooms. They held cards for the public to fill out to report such things as lack of rest room supplies and cleanliness.
Material: Metal
Size: 6" x 4"
Circa: 1960s
Value: $25-$35

Humble rest room comments card box.
Material: Plastic
Size: 6" x 4"
Circa: 1960s
Value: $20-$30

Humble service check card box. These boxes held cards for customers to fill out to let the service station operator know if they were doing a good job or not.
Material: Metal
Size: 6" x 4.75"
Circa: 1950s
Value: $25-$35

Humble brass locks.
Manufacturer: Wilson-Bohannon
Circa: 1950s
Value: $50-$75

Humble sample bottles.
Circa: 1930s
Value: $15-$25 each

Humble map rack.
Size: 11" x 8"
Circa: 1950s
Value: $50-$75

Humble hat badge.
Size: 3" x 2.5"
Circa: 1940s
Value: $200-$300

Humble oval coin bank.
Material: Plastic
Size: 5.75" x 4"
Circa: 1950s
Value: $40-$60

Humble pocket watch.
Circa: 1930s
Value: $100-$150

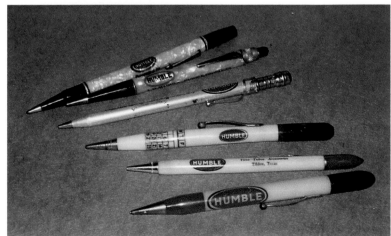

Humble mechanical pencils.
Circa: 1930s-1940s
Value: $25-$50

Chapter 4

Other Jersey Standard Family Members

Enco

Beginning in 1960, Humble introduced a new name in a "few localized test markets"—ENCO, which stood for ENergy COmpany. This was an attempt to find a company name that could be used all across the country. The test went fine and on May 12, 1961, Humble completed the change to Enco in twenty-one states, primarily in the southwestern and central regions. They combined those smaller companies purchased in the '40s and '50s, which included Carter Oil Company, Pate Oil Company, Oklahoma Oil Company and others, into one brand for ease of identification. In nineteen of the twenty-one states, Humble products also carried the Enco name, while in Texas and Ohio Humble products were sold under the Humble name. On the East coast, the company continued to market under the name Esso. The company was therefore still using three brand names to market its products, which was not considered satisfactory. Enco continued to be used until the company made a bold decision to break away completely and on January 1, 1973 it became officially known, as it is today, as Exxon.

This is a typical Enco map of the 1960s when Enco was born.

Enco cans.
Size: 1-quart
Circa: 1960s
Value: $10-$20

Enco Uniflo Motor Oil cans. This was the premium grade motor oil sold in Enco country. The can on top was the first Enco Uniflo and the one on the lower right was the last. This can also has a 5-quart mate, which was the only rollover 5-quart from the 1950s. Cars began to require only 4-quarts, therefore the company decided to produce 4-quart mates to the standard 1-quart cans instead.
Size: 1-quart
Circa: 1960s-1973
Value: $10-$20

Enco cans.
Size: 1-quart
Circa: 1960s-1970s
Value: $10-$20

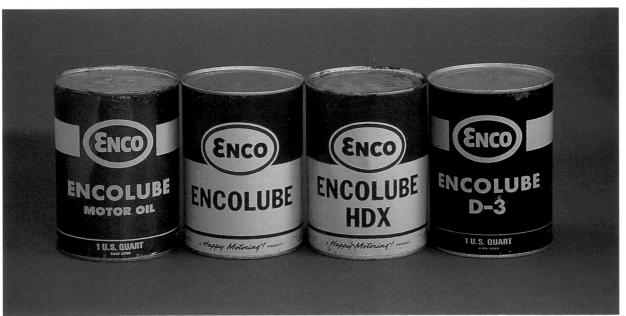

Encolube Motor Oil cans. In November, 1965 Standard Oil Company increased the width of its oval. Therefore, if your can has a "Narrow Band" it was produced before 1965. If it is a "Wide Band" variety, it was produced after 1965. The two cans in the middle of this picture are regular or "Narrow Band" produced before 1965. The two end cans are "Wide Band" produced after 1965.
Size: 1-quart
Circa: 1960s
Value: $10-$20

155

Enco Turbo Oil TJ-37. This was a synthetic jet engine oil. All Turbo Oil is packaged in metal cans, even today.
Size: 1-quart
Circa: Before 1965
Value: $25-$35

Enco Uniflo Motor Oil can.
Size: 4-quart
Circa: Before 1965
Value: $25-$35

Enco Aviation Oil E. This was an ashless dispersant oil designed for piston engines.
Size: 1-quart
Circa: After 1965
Value: $15-$30

Enco Uniflo Motor Oil can.
Size: 1-quart
Circa: After 1965
Value: $25-$35

Enco Aviation cans.
Size: 1-quart
Circa: After 1965
Value: $15-$35

Enco Uniflo Motor Oil plastic can. This was an experimental can material that was tried in the 1965 time frame. Only quarts were produced.
Size: 1-quart
Circa: 1965
Value: $25-$35

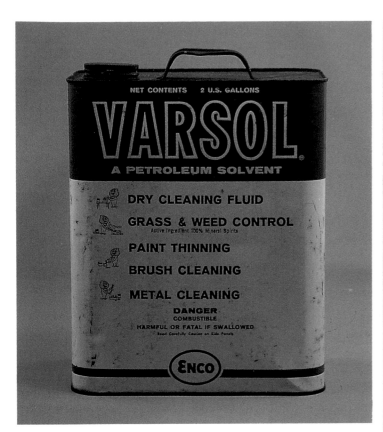

Enco Varsol.
Size: 1-gallon
Circa: 1960s
Value: $20-$30

Above: Enco Product can.
Size: 5-gallon
Circa: After 1965
Value: $25-$35

Below: Enco Perfect Flame Range Oil.
Size: 5-gallon
Circa: Before 1965
Value: $35-$50

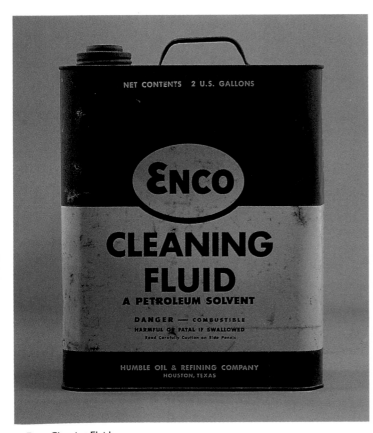

Enco Cleaning Fluid.
Size: 2-gallon
Circa: Before 1965
Value: $25-$35

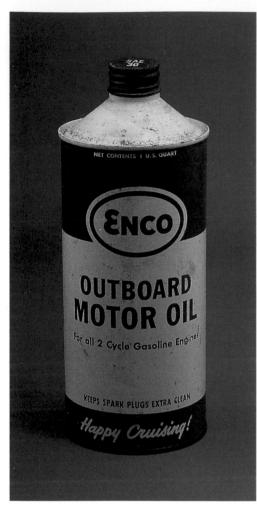

Enco Handy Oil.
Size: 4-ounce
Circa: Before 1965
Value: $15-$20

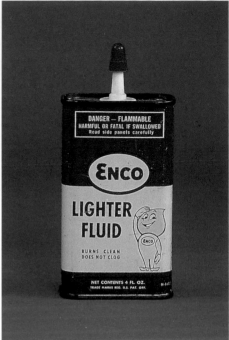

Enco lighter fluid.
Size: 4-ounce
Circa: Before 1965
Value: $15-$25

Enco Outboard Motor Oil.
Size: 1-quart
Circa: Before 1965
Value: $10-$20

Enco Handy Oil. Here are three varieties of cans shown together for easy comparison. They are different because of the oval, which reflects their relative age. The one on the right is the oldest because it has a "Narrow Band" oval. The next oldest is the one in the middle, with the one on the left being the youngest.
Size: 4-ounce
Circa: 1960s
Value: $15-$25

Enco Rust-Ban 392.
Size: 4-ounce
Circa: Before 1965
Value: $10-$20

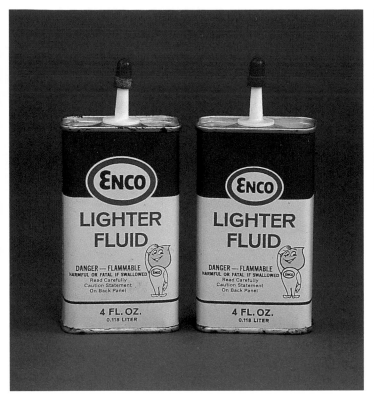

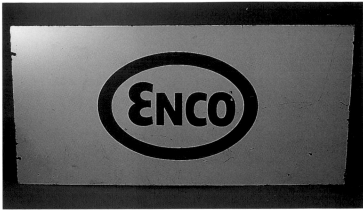

Enco double-sided porcelain sign.
Size: 36" x 17.5"
Circa: After 1965
Value: $150-$200

Enco lighter fluid. Here again are cans together for easy comparison of relative age. Notice the small and large ovals. Both are "Wide Band" so they are after 1965.
Size: 4-ounce
Circa: After 1965
Value: $15-$25

Enco double-sided Atlas Tires sign with Happy Oil Drop.
Material: Plastic
Size: 24" x 21"
Circa: Before 1965
Value: $100-$150

Enco double-sided porcelain Major sign.
Size: 83" x 60"
Circa: After 1965
Value: $100-$200

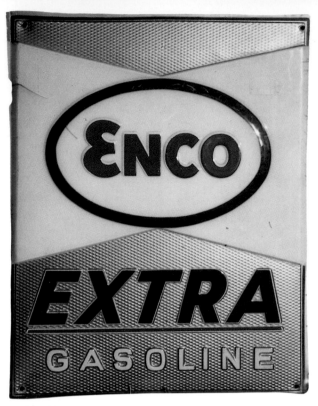

Enco Extra pump sign.
Material: Plastic
Size: 18.5" x 14"
Circa: Before 1965
Value: $50-$75

Enco Happy Oil Drop,
white.
Material: Plastic
Circa: 1960s
Value: $100-$125

Enco watchdog.
Material: Rubber
Size: 43" x 13" x 21"
Circa: 1960s
Value: $700-$1300

Enco rest room key tag holder.
Material: Plastic
Size: 12" x 5.25"
Circa: 1960s
Value: $50-$75

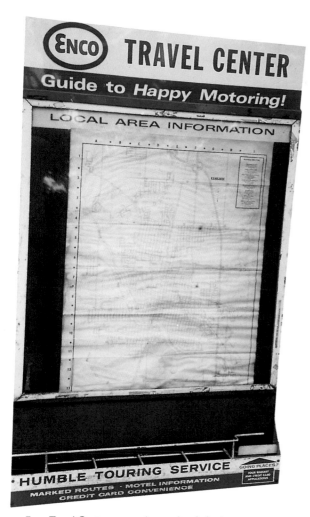

Enco Travel Center map rack, metal and plastic.
Size: 42" x 25.5"
Circa: 1960s
Value: $200-$250

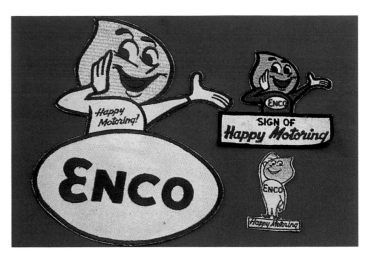

Enco Happy Oil Drop shirt and jacket patches.
Circa: 1960s
Value: $20-$40

Enco shirt and jacket patches.
Circa: 1960s
Value: $10-$25

Enco gas pump glass advertising panels.
Size: 12.5" x 5"
Circa: 1960s
Value: $15-$20

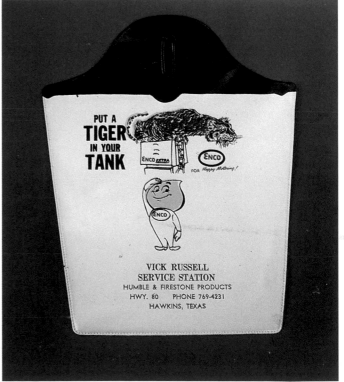

Enco litter bag.
Circa: 1960s
Value: $5-$10

Enco rest room sign with female Happy Oil Drop.
Material: Plastic
Size: 6.25" x 6.75"
Circa: 1960s
Value: $40-$50

Enco first aid kit.
Material: Metal
Size: 8" x 5"
Circa: 1960s
Value: $50-$75

Enco first aid kit.
Material: Plastic
Size: 3.75" x 2.75"
Circa: 1960s
Value: $15-$30

Enco Household Wax.
Size: 1-pound
Circa: 1960s
Value: $5-10

Enco key tender and measuring tape.
Circa: 1960s
Value: Key Tender $25-$35; Tape $15-$25

Enco musical lighter with cloth holder. This lighter plays a song ever time it is lit.
Circa: 1960s
Value: $75-$110

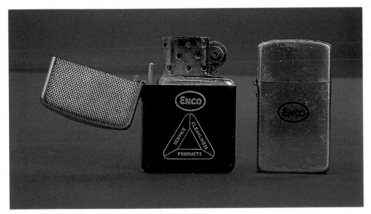

Enco lighters.
Circa: 1960s
Value: $25-$35

Carter Oil Company

The formal incorporation of Carter Oil Company came in April, 1893 but they had been an active producing company prior to that. Carter was founded by Colonel John J. Carter who was born in Ireland in June, 1842 and came to America as a child. He had years of distinguished service in the American Civil War before becoming a merchant and later an oil producer. The company was incorporated in West Virginia during the time it was active in the Sistersville oil field, which had been discovered in 1889. Only a few weeks after this incorporation, sixty percent of the stock was purchased by the South Penn Oil Company, which was owned by Jersey Standard. This made Col. Carter a valuable member of the Jersey family.

Col. Carter was known as a "pungent" speaker and served Jersey in that capacity several times. The company built a refinery in the 1940s at Billings, Montana where they established their headquarters and developed a service station network serving primarily the Northwest. Carter was absorbed into the restructuring of Humble Oil and Refining Company and Esso Standard Oil in 1959; by 1962 all retail outlets were rebranded Enco and today are known as Exxon.

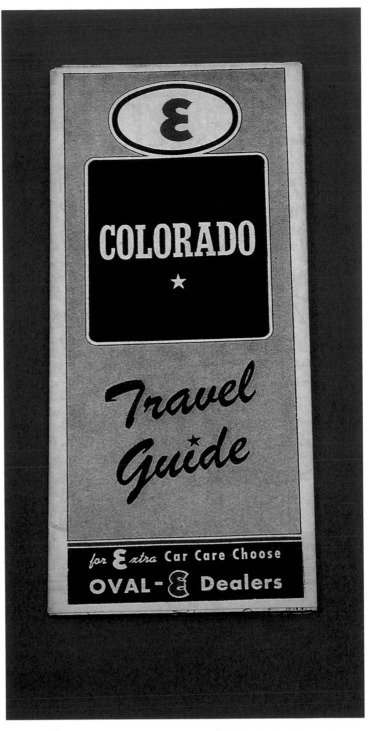

Oval E map. During the late 1940s to 1950, Jersey Standard tried to market in the Carter Oil Company marketing area using the signage of a Greek E in the familiar oval. The US Supreme Court had defined Jersey's marketing territory in the East under the brand name Esso. This logo had such a large following that Jersey tried desperately to push to the West with anything it could that would identify them as Esso without actually defying the Court's decision. Therefore, the single letter E in an oval was tried but was not allowed. As a result, they had to go back to the Carter in the oval.

Carter map.

Oval E porcelain credit card sign, two-sided.
Size: 18" x 14"
Circa: 1940s-1950
Value: $250-$350

Below: Distributors of Oval-E Products, two-sided enamel on metal
Size: 18" x 14"
Circa: 1940s-1950
Value: $150-$250

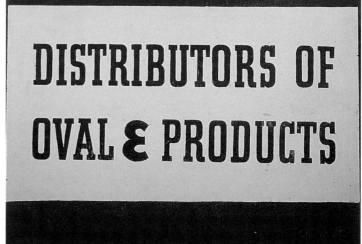

Carter credit card porcelain sign, two-sided.
Size: 18" x 14"
Circa: 1950s
Value: $200-$300

Carter porcelain sign.
Size: 91" x 61"
Circa: 1950s
Value: $150-$250

Carter porcelain sign.
Size: 31.5" x 22"
Circa: 1950s
Value: $250-$350

Carter Happy Motoring enamel on metal sign.
Size: 120" x 30"
Circa: 1950s
Value: $200-$250

Carter Extra Motor Oil embossed sign.
Size: 60" x 24"
Circa: 1940s
Value: $300-$400

Oval E gas pump globe.
Size: 13.5" plastic capco body
Circa: 1940s-1950
Value: $300-$400

Carter gas pump globe.
Circa: 1950s
Size: 13.5" plastic capco; 15" metal band
Value: $300-$400; $450-$550

Oval E Extra gas pump globe.
Size: 13.5" plastic capco body
Circa: 1940s-1950
Value: $350-$450

Carter Extra gas pump globe.
Circa: 1950s
Size: 13.5" plastic capco; 15" metal band
Value: $ 350-$450; $600-$700

Carter gas pump advertising panels.
Circa: 1950s
Size: Carter Extra 11.5" x 5"; Carter 10.25" x 4.25"
Value: $15-$30; $15-$25

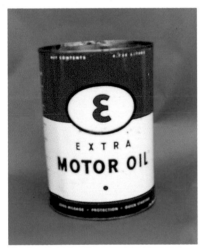

Oval E Extra Motor Oil can.
Size: 1-quart
Circa: 1949
Value: $75-$100

Carter Extra Motor Oil cans.
Circa: 1950s
Size: 1-quart; 5-quart
Value: $20-$30; $35-$50

Carter Motor Oil cans.
Notice that the can on
the left is white and the
can on the right has a
metallic color typical of
others in this family of
cans from the 1950s.
Size: 1-quart
Circa: 1950s
Value: $20-$30 each

Carterlube Motor Oil
Size: 1-quart
Circa: 1930s
Value: No Estimate

Carter oil cans.
Size: 1-quart
Circa: 1950s
Value: $20-$30

167

Carter Motor Cup Grease.
Size: 1-pound
Circa: 1950s
Value: $25-35

Carter Special Engine Oil.
Size: 1-quart
Circa: 1950s
Value: $25-$35

Oval E Motor Cup Grease
Size: 1-pound
Circa: 1950s
Value: $30-$40

Carter Gun Summer Grease.
Size: 1-pound
Circa: 1950s
Value: $25-$35

Carter Gun Summer Grease.
Size: 35-pounds
Circa: 1950s
Value: $30-$40

Oval E Water Pump
Grease.
Size: 1-pound
Circa: 1940s
Value: $30-$40

Oval E Handy Oil Can.
Size: 4-ounce
Circa: 1940s
Value: $50-$75

Carter credit cards.
Circa: 1950s
Value: $30-$60

Carter cigarette lighters.
Manufacturer: Zippo
Circa: 1950s
Value: $35-$45

Carter salt and pepper
shakers with box.
Circa: 1950s
Value: $800-$1,000

Carter sample bottle.
Circa: 1950s
Value: $40-$50

Carter uniform patches.
Circa: 1950s
Value: $5-$25

Colonial Beacon Oil Company

In 1928, Clifford M. Leonard, a promoter, large stockholder, and director of the Beacon Oil Company, was looking for a source of funds with which to meet urgent needs.

Leonard had been a member of the group that started Beacon in 1919. The plan in 1919 was to exploit the possibility of profit by distilling top fractions of Mexican crude to produce fuel oil, for which the Boston area offered a good market. Within a short time, the company had built a refinery at Everett, Massachusetts, acquired tank cars and oceangoing tankers, invested in an oil concession in Venezuela, and built up a marketing system in various areas of New England and New York through an affiliate, Colonial Filling Stations, Inc.

As of November 30, 1928, Colonial Filling Stations, Inc. controlled extensive facilities: it had 354 owned or leased service stations, 4,458 pumps leased to retail dealers, and 77 bulk plants with a storage capacity of 320,000 barrels. The company was overextended and had not paid their stockholders a dividend since 1922. On January 4, 1929, Jersey and officials from Beacon Oil agreed on a plan for Jersey to acquire the major part of Beacon's closely held stock. Jersey had been paying their stockholders a regular dividend, and the Beacon stockholders agreed to the takeover. By the end of January, 1929, Jersey had acquired more than seventy-five percent of the total outstanding shares. Now Jersey had recovered a marketing area that had been taken away from them and given to the Standard Oil Company Of New York by the Supreme Court in 1911. Beacon's name was changed to Colonial Beacon Oil Company in 1934 and remained so until it was absorbed into the Standard Oil Company Of New Jersey in the early 1940s.

Road map. There are no prettier maps than those produced by the Colonial Beacon Oil Company in the 1920s. This is an example of the quality maps they produced during that period. It is not only a map, it details other vital road and sightseeing information to a motoring public that was just beginning to emerge.

Colonial Ethyl gas pump globe. This was the premium grade.
Size: 12.5" x 10"
Circa: 1920s
Value: $500-$800

Colonial gas pump globe.
Size: 15" metal band
Circa: 1930s
Value: $450-$650

Colonial gas pump globe. This was the regular grade.
Size: 12.5" x 10"
Circa: 1920s
Value: $500-$800

Colonial gas porcelain sign.
Size: 48" x 23"
Circa: 1920s
Value: $300-$350

Colonial porcelain sign.
Size: 49" x 23"
Circa: 1930s
Value: $200-$275

Colonial Ethyl two-sided porcelain sign.
Size: 30" x 25"
Circa: 1930s
Value: $500-$600

Colonial Gasoline enamel on metal wooden framed sign.
Size: 51" x 31"
Circa: 1920s
Value: $450-$550

Colonial Gas porcelain sign.
Size: 48": x 10"
Circa: 1920s
Value: $300-$400

Colonial Gas porcelain sign.
Size: 49" x 23"
Circa: 1930s
Value: $200-$250

Beacon Oil Company porcelain sign,
two-sided.
Size: 49" x 14.5"
Circa: 1920s
Value: $175-$250

Beacon, The Oil With the Better
Body porcelain sign.
Size: 48" x 23"
Circa: 1920s
Value: $350-$450

Beacon Oil porcelain sign.
Size: 30"
Circa: 1920s
Value: $500-$600

Beacon Oils porcelain pump sign, curved.
Size: 12" x 10"
Circa: 1920s
Value: $400-$500

Beacon Oils porcelain pump sign, flat.
Size: 9.5" x 9"
Circa: 1920s
Value: $400-$500

Beacon Penn Motor Oil porcelain sign.
Size: 30" x 30"
Circa: 1920s
Value: $250-$350

Colonial Beacon Oil Company

Colonial Beacon Oil Company porcelain sign. This sign represents the combining of the Colonial Gas Company, which only sold fuels, and the Beacon Oil Company, which only sold lubricants. Both became part of Jersey Standard's strategy to increase its market share in the important New England states.
Size: 49" x 14.5"
Circa: 1935
Value: $375-$500

Beacon Penn Motor Oil can.
Size: 1-gallon
Circa: 1920s
Value: $100-$125

Actol Motor Oil.
Size: 2-gallon
Circa: 1930s
Value: $35-$50

Pate Oil Company

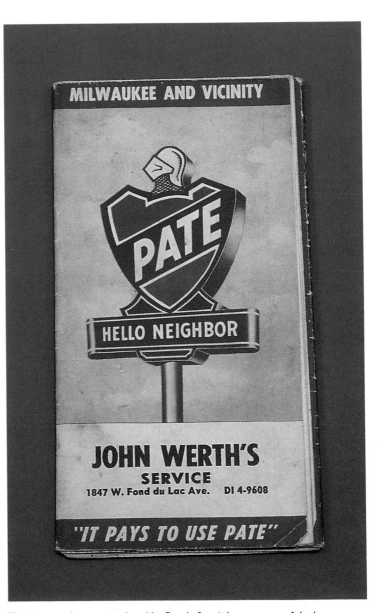

This is a map that was produced by Pate before it became part of the Jersey family of companies. The slogan was a friendly one: "Hello Neighbor / It Pays To Use Pate."

Pate Oil Company was established in Milwaukee, Wisconsin on April 1, 1933—April Fool's Day in the very heart of the depression. The original founders believed that the best way to succeed in the oil business was to sell better petroleum products than any competitor and they put up their last dollar to achieve that goal. They set up their original office in a stable, and obtained office supplies when one of their early large accounts failed and paid them off with bookkeeping supplies. Although this was a time when banks were closing and thousands of other businesses were going bankrupt, Pate distinguished itself in the field of industrial lubricants and fuels and soon gained a reputation as a reliable and capable supplier to the metalworking industry, which was very active in the Milwaukee area at that time. Beginning in 1936, they established a retail marketing network. At the same time they introduced Benzol-Blended gasoline products and for many years Pate was able to offer motor fuel of a higher octane rating than any of its competitors. They were the first with higher octanes, starting with three grades of gasoline and at one time marketing four. They were first with anti-stalling and anti-icing gasoline and first with a cleaner burning fuel. Pate became a member of the Jersey family in 1956.

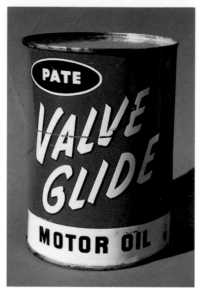

Pate Valve Glide Motor Oil.
Size: 1-quart
Circa: 1940s
Value: $30-$35

Pate Valve Glide Motor Oil.
Size: 5-quart
Circa: 1940s
Value: $75-$100

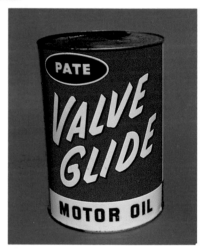

This is a map produced by Pate after their merger with Jersey Standard.

Pate Aqua Glide Outboard and Power Mower Motor Oil.
Size: 1-quart
Circa: 1950s
Value: $50-$75

Pate Motor Oil bottle opener. This was used during World War II to open the caps on motor oil bottles that were in use during that time.
Material: Nickel Plated Brass
Circa: 1940s
Value: $40-$60

Pate memo pad.
Circa: 1950s
Value: $5-$10

Oklahoma Oil Company

The Oklahoma Oil Company was the largest of three companies to merge with Humble in 1959. It was organized in Chicago, Illinois in 1936 as a retail gasoline and fuel oil marketer with eighteen service stations and a combination office and warehouse building. Its name, however, dates back to an earlier and smaller company known as the Oklahoma Oil Products Corporation, which was established at a time when most of the Midwest's oil supply came from the state of Oklahoma.

The mid-1950s saw the Oklahoma brand name gain wide popularity in the sports-conscious Midwest markets after the company began to sponsor television broadcasts of major league baseball games. During this time, Oklahoma Oil Company, along with another progressive Chicago sales organization called Perfect Power Corporation, became members of the Jersey family. In 1958, Oklahoma Oil Company merged with Gaseteria, Inc., a well-rounded retail marketing organization with 263 retail outlets and all became part of the Humble Oil & Refining Company in 1959.

This is a map from the Oklahoma Oil Company before they merged with Jersey. Notice the slogan Happy Motoring To You. Was this an attempt to horn in on Esso's slogan Happy Motoring! that had been registered since 1935?

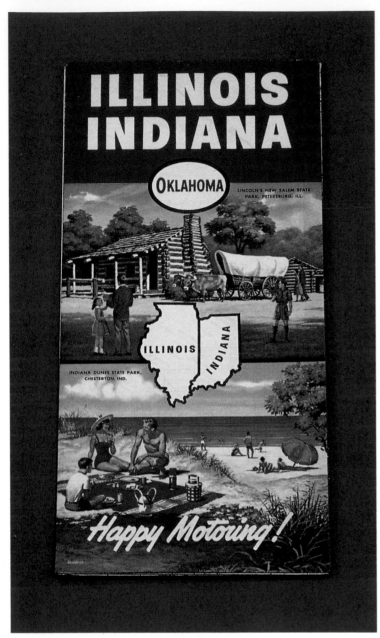

This is a map produced after the merger with Jersey.

Right: Oklahoma High-Q Extra gas pump sign.
Material: Plastic
Size: 18.5 x 14"
Circa: 1950s
Value: $50-$75

Below: Oklahoma Super Power Motor Oil can. This was a can used by Oklahoma before the merger.
Size: 2-gallon
Circa: 1940s
Value: $50-$75

Oklahoma High-Q gas pump sign.
Material: Plastic
Size: 18.5" x 14"
Circa: 1950s
Value: $50-$75

Oklahoma uniform patch.
Size: 3" x 1.5"
Circa: 1950s
Value: $5-$10

Oklahoma Outboard and Power Mower Motor Oil can.
Size: 1-quart
Circa: 1950s
Value: $35-$50

Skelly Oil Company

Skelly Oil Company was a western states marketer that Jersey Standard sold products to for resale in those states that Jersey could not enter with their own brand. Jersey sold Skelly packaged products with a slightly different label and Skelly acted as a distributor for Jersey. In some cases Skelly's name appears on the container as a distributor. In other cases it does not. But we still know from the style of the label and where the item was found that it was a product that Skelly sold. Uniflo Motor Oil is an example of this.

Uniflo Motor Oil bottle. This bottle is not identified any other way other than Uniflo. There is no manufacturer's name on the paper label nor is Skelly identified on the bottle. However, we know this is the same label that appears on another bottle of this period but which has the familiar Esso oval on it.
Size: 1-quart
Circa: 1940s
Value: $50-$75

Opposite page:
Bottom right: Oklahoma credit cards. The one at the bottom was before the merger and is dated 1958. The one on the left was used about 1960. The one on the right is dated 1961.
Material: Plastic
Circa: 1958-1961
Value: $25-$50

Uniflo Motor Oil can
with Skelly Oil
Company Distributors
listed on the front.
Size: 1-quart
Circa: 1930s
Value: $30-$40

Enjay

This was Standard Oil Company of New Jersey's chemical company.

Standard Alcohol Company. This was the early name for Jersey's chemical company which eventually became known as Enjay Chemical Company.
Size: 5-gallon
Circa: 1920s
Value: $35-$50

Uniflo Motor Oil can.
Skelly is not identified.
Size: 5-quart
Circa: 1930s
Value: $30-$40

Uniflo Motor Oil can. This is the first round
factory filled motor can used by Jersey Standard
and it has Skelly's name where you would expect
to find Standard Oil Company Of New Jersey. This
can was introduced in 1934.
Size: 1-quart
Circa: 1934
Value: $100-$125

Enjay Rust-Ban aerosol cans.
Size: 11-ounce
Circa: 1960s
Value: $10-$15 each

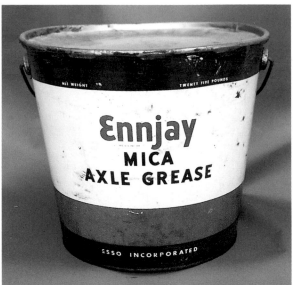

Ennjay Mica Axle Grease.
Size: 25-pounds
Circa: 1930s
Value: $75-$150

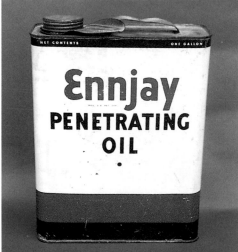

Ennjay Penetrating Oil.
Size: 1-gallon
Circa: 1930s
Value: $75-$150

Penola

Penola Flit Double Action Insect Spray.
Size: 1-pint
Circa: 1950s
Value: $20-$30

Ennjay Mica Axle Grease.
Size: 1-pound
Circa: 1930s
Value: $25-$30 Each

In 1885, Grant McCargo, son of a well-to-do businessman in Pittsburgh, formed a partnership with one Walter Dimock to manufacture a "hot-neck" grease for use in iron and steel, rolling, and tin plate mills. Originally devised to compete with Batson's, an English grease, the "hot-neck" product of McCargo & Dimock became the cornerstone of the business. In 1890, Dimock sold his interest in the partnership and McCargo formed another under the name of Pennsylvania Lubricating Company (Penola). An agreement with Standard Oil Company five years later led to the organization of a fifty thousand dollar corporation using the second partnership's name, with McCargo holding forty percent interest and Standard Oil the remainder. The contract provided that the Pennsylvania Lubricating Company, Inc. should have the exclusive right within the Standard Oil Group to manufacture and sell greases to rolling, tin plate, steel, nail, and sheet mills in the United States, while all petroleum products needed in the manufacture were to be purchased from Standard Oil Companies. Thus began the Pittsburgh Grease Works of the Esso Standard Oil Company.

Standard Oil Company of Louisiana

Between 1906 and 1908 Jersey considered and decided to build a new refinery on the Gulf Of Mexico. Standard Oil officials decided to build this new facility at Baton Rouge, Louisiana and to connect it with the oil fields in Oklahoma via a trunk pipeline. In April 1909, the Standard Oil Company Of Louisiana (Stanocola) was organized. Under the presidency of Fredrick W. Weller, the new company immediately started to build the new refinery and to construct the pipeline north to the Arkansas border where it would meet an eight inch pipe being laid by Prairie Oil across the latter state. The new company was formed for producing, transporting, refining, and marketing. It lasted until January 1, 1945 at which time it was merged into the Standard Oil Company of New Jersey.

Palubco Motor Oil. Penola tried to market their own motor oil independent of Jersey. Since they had an agreement with Jersey to make and sell to jobbers as long as their petroleum oil was purchased from Jersey, they made this motor oil. They had made the first factory sealed canned motor oil for Esso so they had the technology.
Size: 1-quart
Circa: 1930s
Value: $25-$30

Stanocola Gasoline metal band gas pump globe.
Size: 15"
Circa: 1920s
Value: $700-$1,000

Uniflo Motor Oil porcelain rack sign.
Size: 18" x 10"
Circa: 1930s
Value: $100-$125

"Standard" Kerosene Authorized Dealer double-sided porcelain flanged sign.
Size: 21" x 16"
Circa: 1920s
Value: $250-$350

Stanocola Household Lubricant can with shipping crate.
Circa: 1920s
Size: Can 4-ounce; Crate 11.5" x 8.5" x 4"
Value: $200-$300; $35-$55

Stanocola Polarine road sign.
Size: 47.5" x 47.5"
Circa: 1920s
Value: $100-$200

"Standard" Liquid
Gloss can.
Size: 1-gallon
Circa: 1920s
Value: $25-$50

Stanocola Petroleum Products
round porcelain sign.
Size: 18"
Circa: 1920s
Value: $400-$500

Below: Stanocola
Polarine one-sided
porcelain sign.
Size: 36" x 18"
Circa: 1920s
Value: $150-$300

Stanocola Polarine calendar.
Size: 21" x 15"
Circa: 1925
Value: $75-$100

Stanocola Polarine Heavy XX can.
Size: 5-gallon
Circa: 1920s
Value: $75-$125

Stanocola Polarine medium can with crate.
Circa: 1920s
Size: Can 5-gallon; Crate 12" x 10.5" x 15"
Value: $75-$125; $40-$50

Standard Cream Separator
Oil can.
Size: 5-gallon
Circa: 1920s
Value: $35-$50

Bibliography

Gibb, George S., and Evelyn H. Knowlton. *The Resurgent Years 1911-1927*. New York: Harper & Brothers, 1956.

Hidy, Ralph W., and Muriel E. Hidy. *Pioneering in Big Business 1882-1911*. New York: Harper & Brothers, 1955.

Larson, Henrietta M., Evelyn H. Knowleton, and Charles S. Popple. *New Horizons History of Standard Oil (New Jersey) 1927-1950*. New York: Harper & Row, 1971.

Larson, Henrietta M., and Kenneth W. Porter. *History of Humble Oil & Refining Company, A Study In Industrial Growth*. New York: Harper & Brothers, 1959.